P9-EMQ-094

The Rise and Fall of the City of Mahagonny

and

The Seven Deadly Sins of the Petty Bourgeoisie

Works of Bertolt Brecht
published by
Arcade

The Caucasian Chalk Circle

The Good Person of Setzuan, adapted by Tony Kushner

The Good Person of Szechwan

The Good Person of Szechwan, Mother Courage and Her Children,
and *Fear and Misery of the Third Reich*

Life of Galileo

Life of Galileo, The Resistible Rise of Arturo Ui,
and *The Caucasian Chalk Circle*

Mother Courage and Her Children

Mother Courage and Her Children, adapted by David Hare

Mr. Puntila and His Man Matti

The Rise and Fall of the City of Mahagonny
and *The Seven Deadly Sins of the Petty Bourgeoisie*

The Threepenny Opera

The Threepenny Opera, Baal, and *The Mother*

BERTOLT BRECHT

The Rise and Fall of the City of Mahagonny
and
The Seven Deadly Sins of the Petty Bourgeoisie

Edited by John Willett and Ralph Manheim
Translated by W. H. Auden and Chester Kallman

ARCADE PUBLISHING • NEW YORK

The Rise and Fall of the City of Mahagonny copyright © 1927 by Universal-Edition A.G., renewed in 1955 by Bertolt Brecht
The Seven Deadly Sins copyright © 1959 by Suhrkamp Verlag, Frankfurt am Main
Translation copyright for the plays and texts by Brecht © 1979 by Stefan S. Brecht
Introduction and notes copyright © 1988 by Methuen London Ltd.

All rights reserved. No part of this book may be reproduced in any form or by any electronic or mechanical means, including information storage and retrieval systems, without permission in writing from the publisher, except by a reviewer who may quote brief passages in review.

FIRST ARCADE PAPERBACK EDITION 1996

The Rise and Fall of the City of Mahagonny was originally published in German under the title *Mahagonny*. *The Seven Deadly Sins of the Petty Bourgeoisie* was originally published in German under the title *Die sieben Todsünden der Kleinbürger.*

"Notes to my opera *Mahagonny*" and "Introduction to the prompt-book of the opera *Mahagonny*" by Kurt Weill, pages 91–95, reproduced by courtesy of Lotte Lenya-Weill. "Suggestions for the stage realisation of the opera The Rise and Fall of the City of Mahagonny" by Kurt Weill and Caspar Neher, pages 95–99, reproduced by courtesy of Lotte Lenya-Weill and the Estate of Caspar Neher.

ISBN 1-55970-279-6
Library of Congress Catalog Card Number 94-10421
Library of Congress Cataloging-in-Publication information is available.

Published in the United States by Arcade Publishing, Inc., New York
Distributed by Little, Brown and Company

10 9 8 7 6 5 4 3 2 1

CCP

PRINTED IN THE UNITED STATES OF AMERICA

CAUTION

These plays are fully protected by copyright. All inquiries concerning the rights for professional or amateur stage production and concerning the music for these plays should be directed to Jerold L. Couture, Fitelson, Lasky, Aslan & Couture, 551 Fifth Avenue, New York, NY 10176. Outside of the United States of America, inquiries concerning the rights for professional stage production and concerning the music for this play should be directed to the International Copyright Bureau Ltd., 22a Aubrey House, Maida Avenue, London W2 1TQ, England, and those for amateur stage production to Samuel French Ltd., 52 Fitzroy Street, London W1P 6JR, England. Inquiries about use of any material other than in performance should be directed to the publisher.

Contents

Introduction   vii

THE RISE AND FALL OF THE CITY OF
MAHAGONNY   I
Opera

THE SEVEN DEADLY SINS OF THE PETTY
BOURGEOISIE   67
Ballet

NOTES AND VARIANTS   85
Text by Brecht
  Notes to the opera *The Rise and Fall of the City of*
    Mahagonny   87

Notes by Weill and Neher
  Notes to my opera *Mahagonny*, by Kurt Weill   91
  Introduction to the prompt-book of the opera
    Mahagonny, by Kurt Weill   92
  Suggestions for the stage realisation of the opera
    The Rise and Fall of the City of Mahagonny,
    by Kurt Weill and Caspar Neher   95

Editorial Notes
  1. Songs, Songspiel, opera   100
  2. The opera: notes on individual scenes   103

Introduction

Although the opera *Mahagonny* (to give it its short title) is often placed after *The Threepenny Opera* in chronological arrangements of Brecht's works, in fact it was started almost a year before Brecht began work on the latter, and his general conception of it goes back earlier still. It was *Mahagonny* that inaugurated the collaboration with Kurt Weill, and unlike *The Threepenny Opera*, where Weill was brought in at a relatively advanced stage to set the songs, it was from the first a co-operative venture. *Mahagonny* was *durchkomponiert*, or set to music right through. Not only the song texts but the whole structure was jointly established in such a way as to offer prospects of a more radical kind of work, an 'epic opera' whose form, content and ethos would reflect the considerable area of agreement between two highly original minds.

Like Strauss and Hofmannsthal or Gilbert and Sullivan, Brecht and Weill were in their own way peculiarly fitted for the common task. When they met for the first time in March 1927 the poet was just twenty-nine, and his experience of performing his own songs, often to home-made tunes, had accustomed him to writing for singing; moreover he had been married to an opera singer, Marianne Zoff, for whom he considered writing a libretto. Two years younger, the composer had since 1925 been a most productive writer, contributing regular articles to the new radio journal *Der deutsche Rundfunk* on music and a variety of other cultural topics. In 1924 he had met Georg Kaiser, the one Expressionist playwright respected by Brecht, and had thereafter collaborated with him on two operas; while around the same time he also worked with the poet Iwan Goll who had first proclaimed the death of that school. His marriage too had been to an actress: the youthful Lotte Lenya whose voice was to give its very timbre to so many of their songs.

What first brought these two collaborators together appears to have been the radio production of *Man equals Man* in March 1927, and the enthusiastic review which Weill wrote of it; though it also seems that he knew and admired Brecht's poems. Right away, according to Weill (see p. 91), their conversation turned to 'opera's possibilities' and the notion of 'a paradise city' as a theme echoing (as we can now see) certain ideas which Brecht had had in his head for some time. For even before moving to Berlin in the autumn of 1924 he was using the private codename 'Mahagonny' for some of the crazier aspects of Bavaria (then in the aftermath of Hitler's failed coup), and following this he had written the first three 'Mahagonny Songs' with their vaguely Wild West imagery of *Pokerdrinksalons* and the like; a 'Mahagonny opera' indeed was part of his mental luggage for the move. Though he did nothing to develop this further during the subsequent two and a half years, his new collaborator Elisabeth Hauptmann had studied English and she wrote him the two English-language 'Mahagonny Songs' which have ever since figured among his poems. With her he had started working on two related projects: an opera to be called *Sodom und Gomorrah* or *The Man From Manhattan*, and a radio play called *Die Sintflut* (*The Flood*).

The opera project which the two men instantly began to discuss aimed accordingly to deal with the biblical theme of the Cities of the Plain; but in terms of the *Amerikanismus* prevalent in Germany after the stabilisation of 1923/24. Under the impact of the latter *The Flood* had already become known as *Collapse of Miami, the Paradise City*, for which Hauptmann had made a collection of newspaper cuttings dealing with hurricanes, and which clearly underlay the new scheme from the start. Though nothing is known of Weill's contribution at this initial stage it is already evident that if the outward trappings of the opera were to be modish and up-to-the-minute its message would be a Jeremiah-like warning derived from both men's knowledge of the Old Testament. A solemn moral was to be wrapped in an enjoyably flippant package.

Almost at once there was an interruption. Weill was already an

established contributor to the new music festivals at Donau-
eschingen and Baden-Baden, and in the spring of 1927 he was
commissioned to provide one of a batch of very short operas to be
performed at the latter that summer. This struck him as a perfect
pretext for what he termed 'a stylistic exercise' for the new project,
so before either partner got down to work on the opera proper
the so-called *Songspiel* or *Little Mahagonny* was prepared and performed. This consisted of the five 'Mahagonny Songs' (including
Hauptmann's Alabama and Benares Songs) followed by the unpublished 'Poem on a Dead Man' as a finale; and with Brecht's
participation it was staged in a boxing ring in front of projections
by his friend Caspar Neher. Lenya was one of the singers. The
milieu was mock-American, the characters bearing such names as
Jessie, Bessie, Charlie, Billy and so forth; and this was matched by
Weill's use of the jazz idiom, which took one or two of Brecht's
own tunes as a jumping-off point. The other works presented at
the same time were by Milhaud, Hindemith and Ernst Toch,
Hindemith being the festival's principal moving spirit. His contribution *Hin und Zurück*, in which music and action alike run
backwards from a midway point, was based on a Berlin revue
sketch.

The Little Mahagonny was a success, even though there seems to
have been no question of performing it elsewhere. After the show,
in Lenya's words,

> suddenly I felt a slap on the back, accompanied by a booming
> laugh: 'Is here no telephone?' It was Otto Klemperer. With
> that, the whole room was singing the Benares Song, and I knew
> that the battle was won.

This came at a moment when the 'New Objectivity' of the painters
(formally launched in the *Neue Sachlichkeit* exhibition of 1925)
seemed to be merging in a wider movement of a down-to-earth,
deliberately impersonal yet socially critical kind, of which *Amerikanismus* with its cult of jazz and sport formed part. Novel as their
contribution was, Weill and Brecht were by no means alone in this,
for Ernst Křenek's jazz opera *Jonny spielt auf* had already been

performed at Leipzig at the beginning of 1927, and a whole new wave of *Zeitopern* or 'operas of the times' was to follow. Soon the critic Herbert Ihering was writing of Brecht as part of a modern musical-theatrical complex stretching from Chaplin and Piscator to the experiments of Klemperer, Hindemith and Weill: 'All that has hitherto been running along parallel or divergent paths is now joining up.... The age of isolation is over.'

After the summer holidays the three collaborators – for from now on Neher was a vital part of the team – got down to serious work on the opera libretto, which seems to have taken nearly a year. Their aim was to create an 'epic opera' of a new kind, in which a sequence of self-contained musical units would correspond to a 'step by step juxtaposition of situations' on the model (evidently) of *Man equals Man*. Projections like those used at Baden-Baden would add the third dimension to this scheme, which was based on Brecht's idea of an alternative to the integrated Wagnerian *Gesamtkunstwerk*: the new principle which he termed 'the separation of the elements'. What this amounted to in practice was a variety of montage, the major structural principle of the decade, and so far as Brecht's share was concerned he used his previous writings as the main source of raw material for it. On to the nucleus of 'Mahagonny Songs' used in the *Songspiel* therefore were grafted early poems like 'Tahiti' and 'Lucifer's Evening Song' dating from his youth in Augsburg as well as city poems dating from 1926–27 which reflect his first appalled reactions to Berlin. The hurricane advancing on Pensacola came, complete with its thousand victims and its diagrammatic arrow, from a report in the *Chicago Daily News* of 22 September 1926 which was among the *Collapse of Miami, the Paradise City* material. Leokadia (or Ladybird) Begbick is a self-evident importation from *Man equals Man*, Trinity Moses a quasi-Biblical guide through the wilderness to the Promised Land. Such was the mixture used to provide the required musical 'numbers'.

This work had to be fitted in between a succession of more or less demanding distractions. First of all came Brecht's new role as one of the team of dramaturgs for Piscator's Communist-inspired company at the Theater am Nollendorfplatz, which staged four epoch-making productions in the 1927–28 season. Here he found a highly original approach to the use of film, slide projections and other new technical devices, his work on the *Schweik* production in particular making a lifelong impression on him. Weill too wrote incidental music for one of the productions. Then in the spring came the start of the work on *The Threepenny Opera*, a more or less fortuitous job which had previously hardly figured in Brecht's plans, let alone Weill's, but now took up much of the middle six months of 1928. Its very success disturbed all their projects, not least because of the producer's insistence that the formula must be repeated in 1929, an error of judgement that led directly to the *Happy End* fiasco. Finally came a commission for Weill to write a cantata for the Frankfurt Radio, which resulted in the composition of his *Berlin Requiem* to a further montage of texts by Brecht in November–December 1928.

However, the full *Mahagonny* libretto was completed by the middle of that year, and the understanding between the two men, though never intimate, continued to be good. Brecht still assumed, as he had written in the Baden-Baden programme, that Weill's work was

> moving in the same direction as those artists in every field who foresee the collapse of 'society' art . . . It is already addressing an audience which goes to the theatre naïvely and for fun.

– while Weill for his part told the music magazine *Melos* that

> there is no ground whatsoever for the frequently voiced fear that any collaboration with literary figures of real stature must make the relationship between music and text into one of dependence, subordination or at best parity. The more powerful the writer, the greater his ability to adjust himself to the music . . .

The libretto once finished, Weill composed the music during the run of *The Threepenny Opera*, sending off both script and score to his Viennese publishers Universal-Edition in April 1929. The latter had already warned him that the new work looked like being both controversial and financially hazardous to stage, and now they became even more alarmed at the sight of Brecht's text for the brothel scene (the original text, that is, as given on pp. 111–2). On being told by their director Alfred Hertzka that any established opera house would certainly reject it, Weill agreed after some argument to drop the most outrageous passage; marked the whole 'Mandalay' section, with its depiction of the Men queueing up, as an optional cut; and got Brecht to provide him with the poem of the cranes and the cloud, which he set in 3/8 time as a love duet. Shortly afterwards the two collaborators, who may well by now have come to feel that *Amerikanismus* had become rather hackneyed, agreed as far as possible to eliminate the exaggeratedly 'American' names and allusions in the text, and thereby to make it clear that 'the amusement town [or fun city] of Mahagonny . . . is international in the widest sense' and the satire applicable a good deal nearer home. The Weill–Neher 'promptbook' accordingly carries a warning (p. 95) against creating any kind of 'Wild West or cowboy romanticism', while there is a prefatory note in the full score suggesting the use of German names for the original lumberjack quartet of Jim, Fatty, Billy and Jack or Jake. (This was not, however, in time to affect the piano score, whose first edition retains the American names.)

*   *   *

In the cultural life of the Weimar Republic 1929 was a crucial year: and much of the subsequent history of this opera – and perhaps even of the whole Brecht–Weill collaboration – would have been different if the work had been completed twelve months sooner. For the whole climate in which it had been originally conceived now changed, notable stages in the process being the May Day disorders in Berlin, the death of Stresemann (whose foreign policy ever since 1923 had made quite amazingly few concessions to German nationalism) and the Wall Street crash of October which initiated the world economic crisis. Nationalism now once more asserted itself, to the great advantage of the Nazis; the Communist left went over to a policy of aggressive confrontation, largely directed against the Socialists; while a period of economic retrenchment began which affected every aspect of life. It was at this point that Piscator's resuscitated company at the Nollendorfplatz finally failed, as did *Happy End* at the Theater am Schiffbauerdamm (with Brecht washing his hands of it). So far as *Mahagonny* was concerned the effects were threefold. First of all the opera houses, compelled to economise, tended to cut back on modern works, while Klemperer's Kroll-Oper on the Platz der Republik was actually closed down. Secondly there was a considerable wave of feeling against 'decadent' modern art and music, which the crazier Nazis like Alfred Rosenberg interpreted racially as partnegroid (the jazz influence) and partly a destructive operation by the Jews. Finally Brecht's own attitude to politics and the theatre changed radically as he aligned himself with the Communist Party and began developing the new didactic form known as the *Lehrstück.*

With Brecht apparently losing interest once the opera had gone off to the publishers, it was left to Weill to arrange its production. This might possibly have been undertaken by Piscator, who in March had listed it among the forty works under consideration by his company; but that company died in October. Aufricht too, the impresario of *The Threepenny Opera,* was so angry with Brecht over *Happy End* that it was two years before he would consider another work by him. Thus the choice would probably have been limited to the opera houses even if Universal-Edition had not in any case seen them as the natural and preferred outlet. Here the obvious candidate would of course have been the Kroll-Oper with its truly remarkable record of modern productions, for Klemperer knew both collaborators and had a high regard for Weill's music. But such negotiations as took place with the Kroll must have been prior to the opera's completion. For in July the Prussian government's public accounts committee proposed to abolish the Kroll-Oper altogether, and from that point the latter was doomed.

In the end the choice fell on the Leipzig Opera, where two

previous Weill premières had been staged (likewise Křenek's *Jonny spielt auf*), with a second production to follow at Kassel a few days later. These took place in March 1930, by which time the cultural reaction was well under way, with a Nazi, Wilhelm Frick, actually heading the responsible ministry in nearby Thuringia. Though the Kassel production went calmly enough (after some modifications in the last scene to make its slogans seem less 'communistic') the première proper was interrupted by demonstrators, and from then on the opera became a prime target for such people. Accordingly (to quote David Drew), 'the few music-directors who wished to stage it were anxious to do so only with "closed performances"'.

Fortunately Berlin was different, and right up to the Nazi take-over in 1933 left-wing plays and productions continued to be staged; thus Brecht's own extremely radical re-staging of *Man equals Man* could be seen at the Prussian State Theatre in February 1931 (though it only ran for a few performances). It was Aufricht, then, who came to the rescue of *Mahagonny* by deciding to put it on at the specially rented Theater am Kurfürstendamm at the end of that year, and to do so in a predominantly theatrical rather than an orthodoxly operatic production. Actors were engaged rather than singers, with the fortunate result that Weill had to write a new setting for Jenny's Arietta in scene 5 to allow for Lenya's vocal limitations (it is now the accepted one). Brecht and Neher were nominated as directors, while the conductor was Schönberg's brother-in-law Alexander Zemlinsky, previously Klemperer's number two at the Kroll. Many cuts were made, including the crane duet, the Benares Song, 'God in Mahagonny' and the chorus 'Lasst euch nicht verführen'; the whole scale was reduced and shortened; the orchestra was cut down. To Theodor Adorno, though he had come to think an opera house the proper place for this work, it was the tightest, clearest and musically strongest performance yet, while Lenya too has written of it as something quite unforgettable. This in spite of the fact that Brecht and Weill were on bad terms throughout: so much so indeed that Aufricht underwrote the almost simultaneous première of the former's didactic play *The Mother* in order to distract him from the rehearsals, leaving the more amicable Neher in charge.

*   *   *

Though the collaboration effectively came to an end at this point – its last product, to all intents and purposes, being the writing of the didactic 'school opera' *Der Jasager (He Who Said Yes)* for performance in June 1930 – there were two later exceptions. Both of these appear to have been due to the exigencies of exiled life after the Reichstag Fire of 27 February 1933, when both men left the country. One, the planned musical version of *Schweik in the Second World War* for Broadway in 1943, came to nothing. The other, however, was the ballet *The Seven Deadly Sins* which was written in May 1933 and is also included in the present volume.

This comparatively slight work was commissioned by a short-lived Paris-based company called Les Ballets 1933 backed by the surrealist picture collector Edward James, with his Viennese wife Tilly Losch as its principal dancer; their choreographer was Georges Balanchine. Fairly clearly the commission was prompted by the success of Weill's concert there the previous December, when *Der Jasager* and a very trimmed-down version of *Mahagonny*, with Lenya among the singers, were included in a series called 'Concerts de la Sérénade'. So Brecht joined Weill in Paris that spring and supplied a libretto which was essentially a cycle of songs for Lenya in the old pseudo-American vein. As performed at the Théâtre des Champs-Elysées, with Lenya and Losch as the two Annas, this fell comparatively flat – Serge Lifar calling it 'de la pourriture de ballet' – though it made a great impression on Constant Lambert, who conducted the subsequent performance at the Savoy Theatre in London. To Brecht himself however this excursion into the past seems to have been of little interest, for he subsequently paid no attention to his script and made no attempt to get it published. He made just one amendment: the addition of the words 'of the petty bourgeoisie' to the title; the German phrase being *des Kleinbürgers*, the same words as he added to the title of the early one-act play *The Wedding*.

At least this somewhat minor work shows that there was no irreparable quarrel between the two men. But certainly there was from mid-1930 onwards a growing divergence which discouraged any further work of the originality of *Mahagonny*. This probably sprang in the first place from Weill's inability to follow Brecht in his new commitment to Communism after the spring of 1929; for although they collaborated most fruitfully on two out of the first three of the didactic *Lehrstücke* (Hindemith having composed the other) Brecht thereafter found in Hanns Eisler a quite equally interesting composer who was politically and intellectually more compatible with his changed frame of mind. It was thus Eisler with whom he wrote the most extreme of these pieces, *Die Massnahme* (often known as *The Measures Taken*) which Hindemith and his fellow festival organisers rejected in the spring of 1930 on account of 'the sub-standard nature of its text'. And thenceforward, with some ups and downs, Eisler remained Brecht's closest musical collaborator.

On top of this there was evidently some specific disagreement about *Mahagonny* itself. In his indispensable writings on Kurt Weill David Drew has attributed this to what he terms 'the time-honoured rivalry of words and music', suggesting in particular that Brecht was riled by the one-sidely 'musical' slant of the programme note to the Leipzig première. Whether or not this was the cause, he left the compilation of the 'prompt-book' entirely to his two partners, even though Universal-Edition had announced that he too would take part in it; and he also acted quite unilaterally where the publication of the text was concerned. This seems to have taken place some time in the winter of 1930–31 (the relevant number of his *Versuche* being actually dated 1930), and it showed a number of variations from the version composed by Weill. Among these was the changing of the German name Johann previously proposed for the hero Jimmy, so as to turn the four lumberjacks into Paul, Heinrich, Jakob and Josef. This apparently incomprehensible step has recently been interpreted as a gibe at the Baden-Baden festival organisers Paul Hindemith, Heinrich Burkhard and Jakob Haas, together with a possible allusion to one of the heads of Hindemith's music publishers Schott.

More significantly perhaps, the 'Notes on the Opera' which Brecht wrote for this publication in August 1930 not only differ from Weill's views but indicate a considerable disappointment with the way in which *Mahagonny* had turned out. Meant as an epic opera of a new kind, it had finished up as a 'culinary' one, so Brecht felt (see 87–90): that is to say it resembled the conventional opera whose ingredients, instead of being kept separate, are cooked together for the benefit of an audience of musical gastronomes. In fact this was not a criticism of the work itself so much as of its presentation, which had been left in the first place to the established opera houses. For what Brecht was concerned with, and had doubtless imagined Weill to be concerned with too, was not just the writing of 'an opera' but the transformation of the audience and of the whole theatrical and operatic 'apparatus': that Establishment, in fact, which he now realised to be socially and economically based. The trouble, then, was not so much a basic incompatibility between the two men – for after all they spent their summer holidays together at Le Lavandou in 1931 and supported each other in the *Threepenny Opera* film lawsuit that autumn – as a sense on Brecht's part that Weill, once so full of promise for him, had let him down.

And there was indeed some inconsistency between the collaborators' original concept of the staging and the actual results. Thus the provisions of the 'prompt-book' (whose foreword by Weill appeared two months before the Leipzig première) suggest that the set must be made 'so simple as to be equally well transferable from the theatre to any old platform', with neither emotion, stylisation nor any kind of irony or caricature being added to the bald, almost concert-like delivery of the material with its carefully built-in gests. This extreme economy of approach, reflecting possibly the lessons of the first *Lehrstücke* as well as the experience of the *Songspiel* of 1927, was intended to make very clear the piecemeal structure of the work. At the same time it rested on a systematic concept of 'gestic' writing, acting and composition which was actually formulated in the first place by Weill. Indeed his essay 'On the Gestic Nature of Music', which first appeared in *Die Musik* as early as March 1929 – some two years before Brecht started writing of 'the gest' – plainly reflects the work on *Mahagonny*. This principle of identifying the successive attitudes expressed in a work or a scene or a song, and then communicating them individually in all the separate media involved, underlay the whole Weill–Brecht–Neher collaboration. Each point had to be distinctly made from their three different directions in such a way that the audience could follow the cumulative argument without abandoning what Weill termed 'the calm posture of a thinking being'.

Nothing in the available contemporary accounts suggests that these demands ever came near to being fulfilled, not even in the Aufricht production of 1931. And so Brecht may well have blamed Weill for his willingness to listen to the powerful chiefs of Universal-Edition who had done so much to establish the modern repertoire at the Kroll-Oper and elsewhere, instead of seeking that new audience which goes to the theatre 'naïvely'. He could equally well, for that matter, have blamed himself, for once the libretto was off his hands he seems to have left Weill, and in a lesser degree Neher, to settle the question of where and how it was to be staged. Whatever the reason, the salient fact is that from then on he apparently lost all interest in what, after all, remains a powerful, funny, unusually concise and often quite beautiful text. Simply to read, it is one of his finest works. Yet after the 1931 production he virtually ignored it, never (for instance) once mentioning it in the 'working journal' that sets out his achievements, reflections and preoccupations between 1938 and the end of his life. Certainly he did not view it with anything like the affection which he felt for *The Threepenny Opera*, though the latter was a far less original piece of writing.

*   *   *

The translations in this volume are both by W. H. Auden and his friend Chester Kallman. That of *The Seven Deadly Sins* was made for a new production by the New York City Ballet at City Center on 4 December 1958 under Balanchine, with Lotte Lenya and Allegra Kent as the two Annas. This occurred eight and a half years after Weill's death and two years after that of Brecht. The translation of *The Rise and Fall of the City of Mahagonny* was made in 1960 for a planned American première which in the event fell through. It acquired a certain fame however because the late Hannah Arendt, who had a profound admiration for Auden (though a deeply ambiguous attitude to Brecht), wrote in *The New Yorker* that she knew of 'no other adequate rendering of Brecht into English'. Without going quite as far as this, we can put it forward today as a very good version which not only fits the Weill music but contains a number of recognisable Auden felicities; like the Stern–Auden *Caucasian Chalk Circle* translation it certainly deserves to be made available in this country. At the same time it demands to be treated with some reservations, since it is not entirely free of pulled punches and plain misunderstandings.

Some of the latter – like the references to the *Gardine* or half-height curtain of the German stage directions – are so misleading that they have had to be corrected; some will emerge from a perusal of the notes. But the translators' most debatable decision perhaps concerns the return to a modified form of the original 'American' names as found in the piano score which they used. For while it is true that an American audience hearing them for the first time might find that they help make the text more relevant to its own society, to everybody who knows that the work emanated from the Berlin of the 1920s – i.e. for almost anyone directing or conducting it – they conjure up just that modish *Amerikanismus* which Brecht and Weill wanted to discard. Of course the collaborators themselves had somewhat undermined this good intention by their deliberate return to the 'American' milieu in *The Seven Deadly Sins*, which the New York revival further emphasised by consciously setting it in the 1920s. But there remains a considerable risk that if *Mahagonny* is staged in English in this spirit it will become dated, historical, fashionably nostalgic and that much easier for us to stomach.

The unpleasant truth is that this work's message, unlike that of *The Threepenny Opera*, remains as valid as ever in a society like our own. For we too live in a consumer civilisation: one that has been intensified, refurbished and in many ways enriched, but remains every bit as money-conscious as that of Brecht's Suckerville, the 'city of nets'. We too have our idealists who feel that once 'Don'ts are not permitted here' the Golden Age will return and all social and economic problems fade into the background. We too are just as loud in our protests against just as muddled a list of things. And so the message must come direct to us, not altered through a 'period' haze.

The important thing, then, in staging this work is to forget all about the Berlin Cabarets on the one hand and the marching storm-troopers on the other, and treat it as simply and directly as its original conception. For Mahagonny is localised neither in Weimar Germany nor in a pseudo-America but in any society which lives in great cities and becomes obsessed with pleasure and the problem of how to pay for it. Its teaching is far closer to that of the great Bible-thumping revivalists than to the idiosyncratic attitudes of Mr Norris and Herr Issyvoo on which our present picture of pre-Hitler Berlin is so largely based; its choruses do not recall the husky voice of Marlene Dietrich so much as the *Dies Irae*. Its warnings therefore are likely to be relevant as long as such societies depend on commercialised distractions, vices and entertainments, and even their permissiveness remains subsidiary to the rule that everything must be paid for. The point is summed up in one of the inter-scene inscriptions which Auden and Kallman for some reason failed to translate: 'SO GREAT IS THE REGARD FOR MONEY IN OUR TIME.' Only when this no longer applies will *Mahagonny* be truly a 'period' work. To present it as such today is an evasion.

THE EDITORS

The Rise and Fall of the City of Mahagonny

Opera

Collaborators: E. HAUPTMANN, C. NEHER, K. WEILL

Translators: W. H. AUDEN and CHESTER KALLMAN

Characters
JIMMY ⎤
BILLY ⎬ *Lumberjacks*
JAKE ⎥
JOE ⎦
LADYBIRD BEGBICK
TRINITY MOSES
FATTY THE BOOKIE
JENNY
Men and Girls of Mahagonny

Founding of the City of Mahagonny

A large lorry in very bad condition comes to a stop in a desolate place.

FATTY: What's up? We must go on.

MOSES: But the truck has broken down.

FATTY: Then we can't go on.

    Pause

MOSES: But we must go on.

FATTY: But there's nothing there but desert.

MOSES: Then we can't go on.

    Pause

FATTY: Then we must go back.

MOSES: But the sheriffs are waiting back there; they know our faces only too well.

FATTY: Then we can't go back.

    They sit on the running-board and light cigarettes.

MOSES: Further up the coast we might strike a gold-field.

FATTY: Maybe. But the coast is too long.

MOSES: Then we can't even go there.

FATTY: But we might strike a gold-field.

MOSES: Maybe. But the coast is too long.

MADAM LADYBIRD BEGBICK *appearing in the window of the driver's cabin*: Are we stuck?

MOSES: Yes.

BEGBICK: Good! Why don't we stay here? As I always say: If you can't get to the top, stay at the bottom. Listen to me.

The people we've met who have seen the gold-fields agree that the rivers don't like parting with their gold at all. It's back-breaking work. That's hardly in our line. But I took a good look at the faces of those fellows and they'll part with their gold all right, I assure you. Men are easier to manage than rivers. This is the spot for us. Any objections? Then that's settled.

In this empty waste is our town founded
And its name is Mahagonny
Which means Suckerville!
FATTY AND MOSES: Suckerville!
BEGBICK:
We will make it a snare
Plump little birds will be eager to enter.
Everywhere men must labour and sorrow
Only here is it fun.
For the deepest craving of man is
Not to suffer but do as he pleases.
That is our golden secret.
Gin and whisky
Girls for the asking.
We'll have a seven-day week: every day a day of leisure;
And the raging typhoon will never bother us here.
No one shall suffer from the blues,
They'll smoke and dream of all the promises of nightfall
And every other day we'll have boxing
With mayhem and knockouts though the fighting is fair.
Stick that fishing-rod in the ground and run up this bit of
Linen so that the ships returning from the gold-coast
Can see us as they pass.
Set the bar up there
Beside that tamarack.

There is our town
This shall be our centre
This is the . . . *As-You-Like-It Tavern.*
The red Mahagonny pennant is run up on a long fishing-pole.
FATTY AND MOSES:
Why, though, do we need a Mahagonny?
Because this world is a foul one
With neither charity
Nor peace nor concord
Because there's nothing
To build any trust upon.

2

Within a few weeks a city had arisen and the first sharks and harpies were making themselves at home

Jenny and six girls enter carrying large suitcases. They sit on their suitcases and sing the Alabama Song.

Oh, show us the way
To the next whisky-bar.
Oh, don't ask why!
For we must find the next whisky-bar.
For if we don't find the next whisky-bar
I tell you we must die!
Oh, Moon of Alabama
We now must say good-bye.
We've lost our good old mama
And must have whisky
Oh, you know why.

Oh, show us the way to the next pretty boy
Oh, don't ask why, oh, don't ask why!
For we must find the next pretty boy
For if we don't find the next pretty boy
I tell you we must die!
Oh, Moon of Alabama
We now must say good-bye.
We've lost our good old mama
And must have boys
Oh, you know why!

Oh, show us the way to the next little dollar!
Oh, don't ask why, oh, don't ask why!
For we must find the next little dollar
For if we don't find the next little dollar
I tell you, we must die!
Oh, Moon of Alabama
We now must say good-bye.
We've lost our good old mama
And must have dollars
Oh, you know why.
They go out with their suitcases.

3
News of the founding of a new Jerusalem reached the big cities

On the backcloth appears a projection showing a view of a metropolis and a photomontage of men's faces.

MEN:
  We dwell in large dark cities: miles of sewers below them;
  Thick over them, smoke; in them nothing at all.
  No peace, no joy: here is no soil to grow them;
  Here we quickly fade. More slowly they also shall fall.
  Fatty and Moses enter with placards.
FATTY: Far from the hullaballoo . . .
MOSES: – The big express-trains never bother us –
FATTY: . . . Lies our Joytown, Mahagonny.
MOSES: They just were asking where you've been so long.
FATTY: We live in an age that produces many city-dwellers
  city life does not content: all are flocking to Mahagonny,
  the Joytown.
MOSES: Chips and chippies are cheaper!
FATTY:
  Here in all your cities there is so much noise
  So much ill-temper and discord
  And nothing to build your trust upon.
MOSES: For yours is a foul world.
FATTY AND MOSES:
  But once you puff with fellow
  Mahagonny-dwellers
  Smoke-rings white as snow

Soon you'll feel your parchment-yellow
Cheeks glow.
Sky-blue reflections turn
Gold in your drink:
Should San Francisco burn
All there for which you yearn
Must, good or evil, churn
Down the same sink.

MEN *offstage*:
We dwell in large dark cities: miles of sewers below them;
Thick over them, smoke; in them nothing at all.
No peace, no joy: here is no soil to grow them;
Here we quickly fade. More slowly they also shall fall.

FATTY: Then off to Mahagonny!

MOSES: They just were asking where you've been so long.

4

The next few years saw the discontented from every country making their way towards Mahagonny

Jim, Jake, Bill and Joe enter carrying suitcases.

Off to Mahagonny
Where all the winds refresh
Where gin and whisky rivers flow
Past horse- and woman-flesh!
Green and lovely
Moon of Alabama
Shine for us!

Underneath our shirts we've got
Money and we've got a lot
That should smear some smile across
Your big and stupid face.

Off to Mahagonny
Where all the trade-winds blow
Where steaks are cut and blood runs out
But no one runs the show!
Green and lovely
Moon of Alabama
Shine for us!
Underneath our shirts we've got
Money and we've got a lot
That should smear some smile across
Your big and stupid face.

Off to Mahagonny
On swift and even keel
Where civ-civ-il-i-sation
Will lose its scab and heal.
Green and lovely
Moon of Alabama
Shine for us!
Underneath our shirts we've got
Money and we've got a lot
That should smear some smile across
Your big and stupid face.
The men go out.

5

One day there came to Mahagonny among
others a man called Jimmy Gallagher. We are
going to tell you his story.

*A quay near Mahagonny. Jim, Jake, Bill and Joe are standing before
a signpost that reads: To Mahagonny. A price-list hangs on the
signpost.*

JIM:
    When you arrive some place the first time
    You're a bit out of focus to begin with.
JAKE: You don't know where to go or how to go.
BILL: Who to order around.
JOE: Who to take off your hat to.
JIM:
    It's inconvenient
    When you arrive some place the first time.
    Lady Begbick enters carrying a large notebook.
BEGBICK:
    Gentlemen, welcome.
    Just make yourselves comfy. *Consulting her notebook.*
    So you're the famous Jimmy Gallagher!
    We hear tell of your knife tricks, Jimmy.
    At your bedtime you must always have
    English-made gin and bitters.
JIM: Pleased to meet you.
BEGBICK: Lady – that's short for Ladybird – Begbick.
    They shake hands.
    And for your arrival, John Jacob Smith
    We've put on our party clothes.

JAKE: Nice to know you.

BEGBICK: And you're known as Billy?

JIM *introducing him*: Bookkeeping Billy.

BEGBICK: Then you must be Joe?

JIM *introducing him*: Alaskawolf Joe.

BEGBICK:
>And just to show how glad we are to have you
>Prices will be cut till further notice.
>*She makes changes on the price-list.*

BILL AND JOE *shaking hands with her*: Thanks a million.

BEGBICK: Now you'll want to look into our latest crop of cuties . . .
>*Moses brings in pictures of the girls and sets them up. The pictures are like the covers of the old penny-dreadfuls.*
>Gentlemen, every man carries an image of the ideal in his heart: one man's voluptuous is another man's skinny. The way this one can wriggle her hips should make her just about perfect for you, Joe.

JAKE: Maybe that one over there would suit me.

JOE: Actually, I had something a little darker in mind.

BEGBICK: What about you, Billy?

BILL: Me? I pass.

BEGBICK: And you, Jim?

JIM:
>No, pictures don't say nothing to me. I have to pinch them
>   and pat them to know if it's really going to be love.
>Come out, you beauties of Mahagonny!
>We've got the dough, let's see your stuff.

JAKE, BILL AND JOE:
>Seven years we worked Alaska:
>That means frost-bite, that means dough.
>Come out, you beauties of Mahagonny!
>We like to pay for what we like.

JENNY AND GIRLS:
  Here we are to help you melt Alaska:
  Did you freeze there, but make the dough?
JIM: Well, hello, you beauties of Mahagonny!
JENNY AND GIRLS:
  We are the cuties of Mahagonny:
  By paying well, you'll get whatever you like.
BEGBICK *pointing to Jenny*:
  That's the girl for you, John Jacob Smith:
  And if her behind doesn't have bounce in it
  Your fifty dollars won't be worth their weight in toilet
    paper.
JAKE: Thirty dollars . . .
BEGBICK *to Jenny, shrugging her shoulders*: Thirty dollars?
JENNY:
  Have you thought at all, John Jacob Smith
  Have you thought what you can buy with thirty dollars
    now?
  Ten silk step-ins and no change.
  My home is Havana.
  From my mother I get my white blood.
  She often said to me
  'My lamb, don't sell yourself
  The way your mother used to
  For a buck or two.
  You can see what that life has done to her.'
  Have you thought of that, John Jacob Smith?
JAKE: For that, twenty dollars.
BEGBICK: Thirty, sir. We don't bargain. Thirty.
JAKE: Out of the question.
JIM:
  Well, maybe I'll take her.
  You, what's your name?

JENNY:

> Jenny Jones from Oklahoma.
> I've been hereabouts for seven weeks now.
> I was down there in the larger cities.
> I'm game for all things that I am asked to do.
> I know you Jimmies, Jimmies, Jimmies from Alaska well:
> You have it worse in winter than the dead have
> But you get rich in hell.
> In leather jackets and your wallets stuffed with greenbacks
> You come to see what Mahagonny has to sell.
> But this time's not like other Jims:
> They all went crazy for my limbs
> Those limbs belong to you now, baby.
> It wasn't love before to me
> So clasp your hand about my knee
> And drink from my glass too now, baby.

JIM: Good. I'll take you.

JENNY: Bottoms up, handsome.

> *They are on the point of moving off to Mahagonny when some people arrive from that direction, carrying suitcases.*

JOE: But who are these people?

THE PEOPLE WITH SUITCASES:

> Has the ship left?
> No thank God! It's still at anchor!
> *They crowd off hurriedly to the quay.*

BEGBICK *shouting after them*: Bird-brains! Wool-heads! Look at them scuttling off to the ship like a pack of rats! And their pig-skin wallets are still fat with moola! Sons-of-bitches! Blue-nosed baboons!

JAKE:

> I don't get it, why they're going.
> From a fun place, you don't run.
> Do you think that something stinks there?

BEGBICK:
  You boys now, *you're* not going;
  You're coming along to Mahagonny.
  Call it a favour to me
  If you accept another cut in prices.
  She puts a new price-list up over the other.
JOE:
  In this Mahagonny that we'd put so high a price on
  Things are too cheap. That disturbs me.
BILL: To me the place looks too expensive.
JAKE: And you, Jimmy, do you think the place looks good?
JIM: When we're there, it will be good.
JENNY: I used to be so blue before.
THE SIX GIRLS: I used to be so blue before.
JENNY AND THE SIX GIRLS:
  I never could be true before:
  It wasn't you before now, baby.
JENNY, THE SIX GIRLS, BEGBICK, JIM, JAKE, BILL, JOE:
  We know these Jimmies, Jimmies, Jimmies from Alaska
  well:
JENNY AND THE SIX GIRLS: They have it worse in
  winter than the dead have.
JIM, JAKE, BILL, JOE:
  But we got rich in hell.
  But we got rich in hell.
  In leather jackets and their wallets stuffed with greenbacks
  They come to see what Mahagonny has to sell.
  Exeunt for Mahagonny.

6

Instructions

Street map of Mahagonny. Jim and Jenny walking.

JENNY:
One thing I have learned when I meet a gent for the first time, that's to ask him what he is used to. Tell me then exactly how you would like me.

JIM:
As you are, you're exactly my type. If you would call me Jimmy I'd imagine you liked me a little.

JENNY:
Tell me, Jimmy, how would you like my hair done: combed straight or with a wave?

JIM:
They both would look fine to me . . . whatever's the mood you're in.

JENNY:
What are your feelings about underclothes, friend? Should I wear step-ins when I'm dressed or a dress with nothing under?

JIM: Nothing under.

JENNY: As you like it, Jimmy.

JIM: But what would you like?

JENNY: Let's say it's much too soon for me to tell you.

7

Every great undertaking has its ups and downs

On the backcloth is a projection giving statistics about crime and currency fluctuation in Mahagonny. Seven different price-lists. Inside the As-You-Like-It Tavern, Fatty and Moses are sitting at the bar. Begbick rushes in wearing white make-up.

BEGBICK:

Fatty, we're ruined! Moses, we're ruined! Haven't you noticed? People are leaving! They're rushing down to the quay with their bags. I saw them there.

FATTY: What should keep them here – a sprinkling of bars and a deluge of silence?

MOSES: And a fine lot of men they are! They hook a minnow and they're happy; they puff smoke on the porch and they're satisfied.

BEGBICK, FATTY, MOSES:

Our lovely Mahagonny

Has not brought in the business.

BEGBICK: Whisky's down to twelve dollars a quart to-day.

FATTY: By tomorrow it's sure to drop to eight.

MOSES: And sure never to rise again!

BEGBICK, FATTY, MOSES:

Our lovely Mahagonny

Has not brought in the business.

BEGBICK: I've lost all idea what to do. Everybody wants something from me and I've already given them everything. What more can I give to keep them from deserting us?

BEGBICK, FATTY, MOSES:

Our lovely Mahagonny
Has not brought in the business.

BEGBICK:

I, too, was once with a man who took me and put my
Back to the wall:
There we stood and talked for a while
And it was love that we spoke of.
Once all the money went
Talk like that lost its tenderness.

FATTY AND MOSES:

Ready money
Makes you tender.

BEGBICK:

It's nineteen years back that the misery of struggling for
survival began, and it's sapped me dry. This was to be my
last big scheme – Mahagonny, Suckerville. But the suckers
refuse to get caught.

BEGBICK, FATTY, MOSES:

Our lovely Mahagonny
Has not brought in the business.

BEGBICK:

All that's left is to retreat quickly
To follow our steps backwards through a thousand cities
To travel in time backwards through nineteen years, boys.
Pack your luggage! Pack your luggage!
We've got to go back!

FATTY:

Sure, Lady Begbick. Sure, Lady Begbick, we'll go back.
But it's *you* they're waiting for. *Reading from a newspaper.*
'In Pensacola yesterday the county sheriffs arrived in force
and split to pick up Ladybird Begbick's trail. They made a
systematic search of every house and rode off together . . .'

BEGBICK: God! Now nothing will save us!

FATTY AND MOSES:
Dear Lady Begbick,
It's a fact that crime has never paid well
And those dealing in vice do not
Live to grow old!

BEGBICK:
With just a few dollars!
Yes, with just a few dollars
That we might have made in this enterprise
Planned as a snare, which wasn't a snare
I could manage to hold the sheriffs off.
But weren't there some newcomers today?
They looked like money to me.
And maybe they'll spend it with us.

8

Seek and ye shall not find

The quay near Mahagonny. Coming away from Mahagonny, like the people with suitcases in scene 5, Jimmy enters followed by his friends, who are trying to hold him back.

JAKE: Jimmy, what's the hurry?

JIM: What's there to keep me?

BILL: Why that look on your face?

JIM: I'm sick of seeing the word 'Forbidden'.

JOE: But the gin and whisky are so cheap.

JIM: Too cheap.

BILL: And it's so peaceful here.

JIM: Too peaceful.

JAKE: When you feel like eating fish, you can catch one.

JIM: I don't like fishing.

JOE: You can smoke.

JIM: You can smoke.

BILL: You can sleep.

JAKE: You can go swimming.

JIM *copying him*: You can go pick yourself a banana.

JOE: You can look at the water.

Jim shrugs his shoulders.

BILL: You can forget.

JIM: But it won't quite do.

JAKE, BILL, JOE:
   Soft and agreeable is the stillness
   And enchanting is the concord.

JIM: But they won't quite do.

JAKE, BILL, JOE:
   Noble is the simple existence
   And Nature's wonders are sublime beyond compare.

JIM:
   But they won't quite do.
   I think I will eat my old felt hat
   The flavour, at least, will be new:
   And why shouldn't a man eat his old felt hat
   When he's nothing, when he's nothing, when he's nothing
      else to do?

   You've learned to mix your cocktails every way
   You've seen the moonlight shining on the wall:
   The bar is shut, the bar of Mandalay:
   And why does nothing make sense at all?
   You tell me, please, why nothing makes sense at all.
   I think I will set out for Arkansas:

It may not be much, it's true.
But why shouldn't a man go to Arkansas
When he's nothing, when he's nothing, when he's nothing
    else to do?

You've learned to mix your cocktails every way
You've seen the moonlight shining on the wall:
The bar is shut, the bar of Mandalay:
And why does nothing make sense at all?
You tell me, please, why nothing makes sense at all.

JAKE, BILL, JOE:
    Why, Jimmy, must you blow your top?
    This *is* the bar of Mandalay.

JOE: Jimmy says he will eat his hat.

BILL: But why, why should you want to eat your hat?

JAKE, BILL, JOE:
    You mustn't eat your hat, Jimmy!
    We won't let you do that, Jimmy!
    Hat-eating goes too far –
    Eating hats in a bar!
    Shouting.
    We'll give you a beating
    Jimmy! Hat-eating
    'S not what mankind was born for.

JIM *calmly*: You tell me! What is it man was born for?

JOE: Well, now you've said your little piece, you can come
    along with us like a good boy, home to Mahagonny.
    They take him back to Mahagonny.

9

Under a wide-open sky, in front of the As-You-Like-It Tavern, the Men of Mahagonny, including the Four Friends, are sitting on rocking chairs, smoking and drinking. They are listening to a piano, and dreamily watching a white cloud which travels back and forth across the sky. Around them are printed notices bearing such inscriptions as 'Kindly take care of my furniture. L.B.' 'Wipe your shoes before entering. L.B.' 'Do not put your feet on the table. L.B.' 'No spitting. L.B.' 'Ashtrays have been provided: use them. L.B.' 'Do not pick your teeth in public. L.B.' 'Do not throw razor blades down the W.C. L.B.' 'Please refrain from using indecent language and singing indecent songs. L.B.' 'Keep this establishment as we like it and it will be as-you-like-it.'

JIM:
>Deep in the woods of ice-bound Alaska
>Seven winters I toiled with three buddies together
>Cutting down trees and hauling logs through the snow
>And I lived on raw meat and saved my earnings:
>Seven years it's taken to get me
>Here where I now am.

>There in a riverside hut for seven winters
>Carving our curses with our knives in the table
>Talking of nothing but where we would go to
>Of just where we would go to when we'd saved enough
>   money
>Hungered, thirsted, sweated, shivered to
>Get where we now are.

>When our time was over, we picked up our savings.

Out of all towns we had to choose from, we chose
   Mahagonny
Made our way here without stopping to rest
By the shortest route.
And what does it all add up to?
That no fouler place could exist
Nor any duller one be found on earth than
Here where we now are.
He jumps to his feet.
What's the big idea? You think you can treat us like this?
You've got a second think coming. Come out of there, you
As-You-Like-It slut! It's Jimmy Gallagher talking . . . from
Alaska . . . He doesn't like it here!

BEGBICK *coming out of the Tavern*: What don't you like here?

JIM: Your dungheap.

BEGBICK: I seem to keep hearing 'dungheap'. Did anyone by
   chance say
   'Dungheap'?

JIM: You heard me. I said *Dungheap*.
   The cloud shakes and goes quickly off.
   Seven winters, seven winters hauling logs and cutting down
   trees . . .

THE SIX GIRLS, JAKE, BILL, JOE: He spent in cutting down
   trees . . .

JIM: And the rivers, and the rivers, and the rivers jammed
   with floating ice . . .

JAKE: Be quiet, Jim.

THE SIX GIRLS, JAKE, BILL, JOE: The rivers jammed with
   floating ice . . .

JIM:
   Hungered, thirsted, sweated, shivered, Slaving like a beast
      to get here
   But I do not like it here, for

Nothing's going on.

JENNY:

Listen, Jimmy! Listen, Jimmy!

Please be good and put that knife away.

JIM: Hold me, hold me back!

JAKE, BILL, JOE: Please be good and put that knife away.

JENNY:

Listen, Jimmy!

Be a good boy, Jimmy, and behave.

JIM:

Seven years of felling timber

Seven years of cold and squalor

Seven years of bitter toil and

This is all you have to offer:

BEGBICK, FATTY, MOSES: You have quiet, concord, whisky, women.

JIM: Quiet! Concord! Whisky! Women!

JENNY, JAKE, BILL, JOE: Put your knife back in your belt now!

CHORUS: Qui-et! Qui-et!

BEGBICK, FATTY, MOSES: You can sleep here, smoke here, fish here, swim here.

JIM: Sleeping! Smoking! Fishing! Smoking!

JENNY, THE SIX GIRLS, JAKE, BILL, JOE:

Jimmy, put that knife away!

Jimmy, put that knife away!

CHORUS: Qui-et! Qui-et!

BEGBICK, FATTY, MOSES:

We know these Jimmies from Alaska.

We know these Jimmies from Alaska.

JIM:

Hold me, hold me back! Or there will be trouble.

Hold me, hold me back!

JAKE, BILL, JOE:
  Hold him, hold him back! Or there will be trouble.
  Hold him, hold him back!
CHORUS:
  We know these Jimmies, Jimmies, Jimmies from Alaska
    well:
  They have it worse in winter than the dead have.
  But you get rich in hell. But you get rich in hell.
BEGBICK, FATTY, MOSES: Why can't stupid swine like these
  remain forever in Alaska? All they ever want to do is spoil
  the fun of peace and concord. Throw the bastard out! He's
  had enough.
JIM:
  Hold me, hold me back or there'll be trouble!
  For there's no life here!
  For there's no life here!
  He stands on a table.
  No, not all your bars in Mahagonny
  Will ever make a man happy:
  There's too much charity
  And too much concord
  And there is too much
  To build all his trust upon.
  All the lights go out. Everyone remains as he is in the dark.

10

In enormous letters on the backcloth appears: TYPHOON!, *and then:*
A HURRICANE THREATENS MAHAGONNY.

ALL:
  No! Not utter destruction!

Our golden Joytown will be lost!
For the raging storm hangs over the mountains:
We shall die, drown in the waters of death.
We face utter destruction
A black, horrible end!

O is there no wall to shelter us now?
O is there no cavern which will hide us?
We face utter destruction
A black, horrible end!

11

During this dreadful night an untutored lumberjack called Jimmy Gallagher had a vision in which the laws of human happiness were revealed to him

The night of the hurricane. Sitting on the ground leaning against the wall are Jenny, Begbick, Jim, Jake, Bill and Joe. All are in despair, but Jim is smiling. From backstage can be heard the voices of men in procession as they pass behind the wall.

THE MEN OF MAHAGONNY *off*:
    Stout be your hearts though dark be the night
    Stand though the sun and the moon take to flight:
    Hence with idle wailing
    Tears are unavailing;
    Face the fury of the storm and fight!
JENNY *softly and sadly*:
    Oh, Moon of Alabama

We now must say good-bye.
We've lost our good old mama
And must have whisky
Oh, you know why.

JAKE:

Why try to escape it?
It's no use.
To run away
Cannot save you.
The best thing we can do
Is to sit here
And face it
Until the end comes.

THE MEN OF MAHAGONNY *off*:

Stout be your hearts though dark be the night
Stand though the sun and the moon take to flight:
Hence with idle wailing
Tears are unavailing;
Face the fury of the storm and fight!
Jim laughs.

BEGBICK: What's the laugh for?

JIM:

So, then – that's how it is!
Quiet and concord do not exist.
But the big typhoons have existence.
So do earthquakes. You can ignore neither.
And the same is true of mankind:
It must destroy and bring ruin.
You're afraid of raging hurricanes?
You think that typhoons are shocking?
Wait till a man is out to have his fun.

In the distance: 'Stout be your hearts . . .' etc.

JAKE: Be quiet, Jim.

JOE: You talk too much.

BILL: Relax and smoke and forget.

JIM:

> You may build a tower taller than Everest:
> Man will come and smash it to bits.
> He'll do it for the hell of it.
> The straightest way shall be made crooked
> And the high place brought down to dust.
> We need no raging hurricane
> We need no bolt from the blue:
> There's no havoc which they might have done
> That we cannot better do.

In the distance: 'Stout be your hearts . . .' etc.

BEGBICK:

> Bad is the hurricane.
> Even worse the typhoon.
> But the worst of all is man.

JIM *to Begbick*:

> Listen! You've had placards put up
> Upon which was written:
> *This is prohibited.*
> *That you mustn't do.*
> That sort of thing spoils any happiness.
> Boys! In that corner there is a placard.
> It says there: *It is henceforth forbidden*
> *To sing any cheerful songs.*
> But before two o'clock strikes
> You will hear Jimmy Gallagher
> Singing a cheerful song
> To show you that
> Nothing is forbidden.

JOE:

We need no raging hurricane
We need no bolt from the blue;
There's no havoc which they might have done
That we cannot better do.

JENNY:

Be quiet, Jim. You talk too much.
Come outside with me: make love to me.

JIM:

No. I've more to say.

Dreams have all one ending:
To wake and be coldly sure
To see the dark descending
To hear the wind portending
A night that shall endure.

Life, our only treasure
Runs out before you know.
The deepest draught of pleasure
Will seem too short a measure
When you are told to go.

Daily we grow older.
We have but little time
So leave the dead to moulder
To be alive is nobler
To flee from life, a crime.

Take not as your teacher
The tyrant or the slave.
And do not dread the preacher:
The end for every creature

Is nothing but the grave.
He comes to the front of the stage.

If you see a thing
You can only have for cash
Then fork out your cash:
If someone is passing by who has cash
Knock him on the head and take all his cash:
Yes, do it!

If you fancy a lovely home
Then enter a home
And pick yourself a bed:
If the housewife comes, make a twosome with her
If the roof begins leaking, get away!
Yes, do it!

If one morning a thought occurs
New to your mind
Think that, like all thinking
It'll cost you cash and ruin your home:
Think it, though! Think it, though!
Yes, do it!

For the sake of good order
The good of the state
For humanity's future
And for your personal satisfaction
Do it!

*All have risen. They are now holding their heads high. Jim returns
to them and they congratulate him.*
THE MEN OF MAHAGONNY *offstage*:
Hence with idle wailing

Tears are unavailing;
Face the fury of the storm and fight!

BEGBICK *beckons Jim and goes into a corner with him*: So you
think I was wrong to forbid anything.

JIM: Yes. Now I'm cheerful, I feel like tearing down all your
precious notices. Even the walls will have to go. The hurricane won't pay you for them, but I will. Here. Take this.

BEGBICK *to all*:

Let each one do just what he likes,
The storm will soon do it too:
So when a raging hurricane strikes
There's nothing we may not do.

JIM, JAKE, BILL, JOE:

Clap your hands when a hurricane strikes:
Who cares for being immortal?
When a man can do just what he likes
Who's afraid of the storm at his portal?
Let it say
Any day:
Do you think you're immortal?

Fatty and Moses rush in excitedly.

FATTY AND MOSES:

Destroyed is Pensacola!
Destroyed is Pensacola!
And the hurricane roars
On its raging way to Mahagonny!

BEGBICK *exultantly*:

Pensacola!
Pensacola!
The sharp-eyed sheriffs are swallowed up
The just alike with the unjust have been brought to
    nothing:
It must have taken them all!

JIM:

    You are free, I say, if you dare!

    You may do all tonight that's prohibited.

    Soon the hurricane will do it as well, so

    Sing, as an example, for that's prohibited.

THE MEN OF MAHAGONNY *quite close behind the wall*: Be
quiet! Be quiet!

JIM WITH JENNY AND JOE:

    Come on, sing with us!

    Sing with us, sing any cheerful song.

    If it's prohibited

    Sing it with us!

JIM *jumping on to the wall*:

    As you make your bed, so you lie on it

    The bed can be old or brand-new;

    So if someone must kick, why, that's my part

    And another get kicked, that part's for you!

ALL:

    As you make your bed, so you lie on it

    The bed can be old or brand-new;

    So if someone must kick, that is my part,

    And another get kicked, that's for you!

    *Lights out. On the backcloth is a map on which an arrow indi-
cating the path of the hurricane moves slowly towards Mahagonny.*

CHORUS *distant*: Stout be your hearts though dark be the
night!

12

*In a dim light, the Men and Girls of Mahagonny are waiting on a
country road outside the city. As at the end of scene 11, the projection*

on the backcloth shows an arrow moving slowly towards Mahagonny. Every so often during the orchestral introduction a loudspeaker makes announcements: 'The hurricane is now approaching Atsena at a speed of one hundred and twenty miles an hour.'

Second loudspeaker announcement: 'Atsena totally destroyed. No reports coming through. Communications with Atsena impossible to re-establish.'

Third loudspeaker announcement: 'The hurricane's speed is increasing; it is now making straight for Mahagonny. All lines to Mahagonny are now down.
In Pensacola 11,000 are reported dead.'

All are watching the arrow horror-struck. Suddenly, a minute's distance from Mahagonny, the arrow stops. Dead silence. Then the arrow makes a rapid half-circle around Mahagonny and moves on. Loudspeaker:
'The hurricane has veered in a circle round Mahagonny and is continuing on its course.'

MEN AND GIRLS:
O wonderful salvation!
Our lovely city stands unharmed.
The raging hurricane veered away in a new direction
And pale death said to the waters: Go back.
Rejoice in our salvation!

From now on the phrase 'do it', which they had been taught in that night of horror, became the motto of the people of Mahagonny

13

A year later. Mahagonny is booming.

Men step on to the apron and sing.

CHORUS:
One means to eat all you are able;
Two, to change your loves about;
Three means the ring and gaming table;
Four, to drink until you pass out.
Moreover, better get this clear
That Don'ts are not permitted here.
Moreover, better get it clear
That Don'ts are not permitted here!
The Men return to the stage and take part in what follows. On the signs at the back of the stage in enormous letters is the word 'EATING'. A number of the Men, including Jim, are seated at tables laden with joints of meat. Jake, now known as Guzzler, is seated at a centre table eating incessantly. On each side of him, a Musician is playing.

GUZZLER JAKE:
Two calves never made a man fatter:
So serve me a third fatted calf.
All is only half:
I wish it were me on my platter.

JIM AND JAKE:
Always insist on the whole
Never be content with half!

SOME OF THE MEN:
Jake Smith! You're a stout soul!
Eat away! Don't give up! One more calf!

JAKE:

Watch me! Watch me! Would you have guessed
How much one person can eat?
In the end I shall have a rest.
To forget is sweet.
More please! Give me more . . .
He topples over dead.
The Men form a half-circle behind and remove their hats.

MEN:

Smith lies dead in his glory
Smith lies dead in his happiness
Smith lies dead with a look on his face
Of insatiable craving
For Smith went the whole hog
And Smith has fulfilled himself:
A man without fear.
They put their hats on.

MEN *moving along the apron*: Next we change our loves about.

14

The word 'LOVING' in enormous letters is seen on the signs at the back. On a platform, a bare room has been set up. In the middle of this room sits Begbick with a Girl seated on her left and a Man on her right. Below the platform the Men of Mahagonny are queueing up. Background music.

BEGBICK *turning to the man next to her*:

Spit out your chewing-gum, boy.
See that your hands aren't dirty.

Give the girl time:
A short conversation's polite.
MEN *without looking up*:
Spit out your chewing gum, boys.
See that your hands aren't dirty.
Give the girl time:
A short conversation's polite.
The room slowly darkens.

Get to it soon!
Play that Mandalay immortal tune:
Love's not dependent on time for a lover.
Lovers, make haste
Lovers, don't waste
What in seconds is over:
Mandalay won't glow
Forever below
Such a moon.

Lovers, stop waiting
Hurry, the juicy moon
Is green and slowly setting.
*The room has gradually grown light again. The man's chair is now
empty. Begbick turns to the Girl.*
BEGBICK:
By itself, ready money
Won't or can't make you tender.
MEN *without looking up*:
By itself, ready money
Won't or can't make you tender.
The room grows dark again.
Get to it soon!
Play that Mandalay immortal tune:

Love's not dependent on time for a lover.
Lovers, make haste
Lovers, don't waste
What in seconds is over:
Mandalay won't glow
Forever below
Such a moon.

Lovers, stop waiting,
Hurry, the juicy moon
Is green and slowly setting.
The room grows light again. Another Man enters, hangs his hat on the wall, and sits in the empty chair. The room slowly darkens again.

MEN:
Mandalay won't glow
Forever below
Such a moon.
When the stage grows light again, Jim and Jenny are seated on two chairs some distance from one another. He is smoking, she is putting on make-up.

JENNY:
See there two cranes veer by one with another.

JIM:
The clouds they pierce have been their lot together

JENNY:
Since from their nest and by their lot escorted

JIM:
From one life to a new life they departed

JENNY:
At equal speed with equal miles below them

BOTH:
And at each other's side alone we see them:

JENNY:

> That so the crane and cloud may share the lovely –
> The lonely sky their passage heightens briefly;

JIM:

> That neither one may tarry back nor either

JENNY:

> Mark but the ceaseless lolling of the other
> Upon the wind that goads them imprecisely
> As on their bed of wind they lie more closely.

JIM:

> What though the wind into the void should lead them
> While they live and let nothing yet divide them:

JENNY:

> So for that while no harm can touch their haven

JIM:

> So for that while they may be from all places driven
> Where storms are lashing or the hunt beginning:

JENNY:

> So on through sun and moon's only too similar shining
> In one another lost, they find their power

JIM:

> And fly from?

JENNY:

> Everyone.

JIM:

> And bound for where?

JENNY:

> For nowhere.

JIM:

> Do you know what time they have spent together?

JENNY:

> A short time.

JIM:

And when they will veer asunder?

JENNY:

Soon.

BOTH:

So love to lovers keeps eternal noon.
Men move along the apron.

MEN:

One means to eat all you are able;
Two, to change your loves about;
Three means the ring and gaming table;
Four, to drink until you pass out.
Moreover, better get it clear
That Don'ts are not permitted here.
(So long as you have money).

15

The Men go back upstage, where a boxing ring is being set up in front of a background displaying the word 'FIGHTING'. On a platform to one side, a brass band is playing.

JOE *standing on a chair*:

We have the honour today to present the greatest
Fight ever: to be won by a straight Kayo –
The famous bruiser, Trinity Moses
Versus me, the – Alaskawolf Joe.

FATTY:

What! You're challenging Trinity Moses!
Boy! You'd best be making your will.

That's no fight. It's murder. When that man
Enters the ring, he's out to kill.

JOE:

That may be so, but the bid's worth making:
All that I earned in Alaska I'm staking
For I believe that I shall win through.
May all those who have known me longest
Bet upon Joe to prove the strongest.
Jimmy, I'm counting above all on you!
All those who believe more in brains than in brawn
That Jack may be small but the giant is slow –
Victory nearest when hope seems forlorn –
Will lay their bets on Alaskawolf Joe.

MEN:

All those who believe more in brains than in brawn
That Jack may be small but the giant is slow –
Victory nearest when hope seems forlorn –
Will lay their bets upon Alaskawolf Joe!
Joe has gone over to Bill.

BILL:

Joe, we're close as friends, you know –
But it goes against the grain so
Chucking money down the drain, so . . .
I've put my money on Moses, Joe.
Joe goes to Jim.

JIM:

Joe, my brother in work and in play
And my closest friend of any
I am betting on you today
All I have, Joe, every penny.

JOE:

Jim, when you say that, before me
Far Alaska rises up

Those seven winters of bitter weather
When we felled timber, we two together.

JIM:

Joe, my oldest friend, I tell you
All I prize I would give up:
Those seven winters of bitter weather
When we felled timber, we two together.

JOE:

Jim, when you told me you'd dare it
Our Alaska came in view:
The seven winters of bitter weather
When we felled timber, we two together.

JIM:

Joe, I'd sooner lose, I swear it
Than betray that life we knew:
The seven winters of bitter weather
When we felled timber, we two together.
Alaska I see and pair it
Ever, Joe, only with you!

JOE:

You'll win your money, I swear it!
I'll do all a man can do!
The boxing ring is set up by now. Moses enters it.

MEN:

Give three cheers for Trinity Moses!
Good old Moses! Give him hell, man!

A WOMAN'S VOICE *screaming*:
This is murder!

MOSES:

I regret it.

MEN:

Hit him so's he won't forget it!

REFEREE *introducing the fighters*:

(Our) Trinity Moses, two hundred pounds.

Alaskawolf Joe, one-eighty . . .

MAN *shouting*:

Coffee grounds!

Last preparations for the bout.

JIM *from below*:

How you feeling?

JOE *in the ring*:

All set.

JIM:

Keep your end up.

JOE:

You bet.

The fight begins.

MEN *alternately*:

Let's go! Fight, boys!

Shit! Quit stalling!

Now, Joe! No clinches! Foul! Get at it!

More blood! Neat one! Nail him! he's had it!

Watch it! Perfect! Hey! he's falling!

Trinity Moses and Joe are boxing in time to the music.

MEN *together*:

Moses, keep slugging

Make him swallow dirt!

Moses, beat him up, man!

Land them where they hurt!

Moses, a left hook

Now a right as well!

Sock him in the kidney!

Moses, give him hell!

Joe drops to the canvas.

REFEREE *starts counting him out, then*:
> The man's dead.
> *A burst of laughter from the Men. The crowd breaks up.*

MEN *dispersing*:
> A Kayo's a Kayo. He couldn't take it.

REFEREE:
> The winner: Trinity Moses!

MOSES:
> I regret it.
> *Exit.*

BILL *to Jim: they are alone in the ring together*:
> I said he wouldn't make it.
> I warned him he'd get it.
> He has.

JIM *softly*:
> So long, Joe.
> *The Men move along the apron.*

MEN:
> One means to eat all you are able;
> Two, to change your loves about;
> Three means the ring and gaming table;
> Four, to drink until you pass out.
> Moreover, better get it clear
> That Don'ts are not permitted here.
> Moreover, better get it clear
> That Don'ts are not permitted here!

16

*Men are back on the main stage. The signs in the background display
the word 'DRINKING'. The Men sit down, put their feet up on the
table and drink. Downstage Jim, Bill and Jenny are playing billiards.*

JIM:
  Drinks on me. The gang is my guest.
  I just want to show
  That it's easy work at best
  To be knocked out like Joe.
  Lady Begbick, set them up for all the gents!
MEN:
  Good for Jimmy! It's a pleasure! It makes sense!

  Mahagonny sure was swell
  Daily rates were twenty dollars;
  Those who raised more special hell
  Had to pay a little extra:
  Then they all were steady callers
  At Mahagonny's luxury saloon,
  So they all lost their shirts and collars
  But at least they saw the moon.

  Both at sea and on land
  Everyone who gets around is sure to get a skinning:
  That's the reason everybody
  Strips his own skin from his body
  And when pelts are bought on every hand
  With dollars, thinks he's winning!
JIM:
  Lady Begbick, set them up again for all the gents!

MEN:
   Good old Jimmy! Double whiskys! No expense!

   Both at sea and on land
   Skins are up for sale and their consumption is extensive:
   Who's to pay when everybody
   Feeds the tiger in his body?
   For those yellow pelts go cheaply and
   The whisky comes expensive!

   Mahagonny sure was swell
   Daily rates were twenty dollars;
   Those who raised more special hell
   Had to pay a little extra:
   Then they all were steady callers
   At Mahagonny's luxury saloon
   So they all lost their shirts and collars
   But at least they saw the moon.

BEGBICK:
   Time to settle the bill, gentlemen.

JIM *softly*:
   Jenny, come here. Jenny
   I'm out of money.
   We'd better beat it from here;
   It sure makes no difference to where.
   Loudly addressing everyone, pointing to the billiard table:
   Gentlemen, climb on this clipper with me!
   With all of us aboard, we'll put to sea!
   Again softly:
   Spend this ocean trip at my side, Jenny
   For the deck will tremble like the earth quaking.
   You as well, Billy. Don't desert me now.
   We'll go sailing back to old Alaska, buddies

For this is not the place for us.
Loudly.
Now or never we will hoist our sails and head for our
   Alaska!
*With part of the bar-rail, a curtain and various other objects in
the room, a 'ship' is constructed on the billiard-table, which Jim,
Bill and Jenny 'board'. There they take up sailor-like poses.*

JIM:
   Pour cognac down the toilet and flush it
   And latch your salmon-pink persian-blinds:
   Alaska's our goal; we won't have to rush it
   We'll get there on relaxed behinds.
   The Men remain seated below watching them, vastly amused.

MEN:
   Ahoy, Jimmy! Was Columbus greater?
   Ahoy there, how that guy can handle the sails!
   Jenny, get undressed. It's too hot. The Equator!
   Stay buttoned, Billy. The Gulf Stream gales!

JENNY: O God! Isn't that a typhoon to starboard?

MEN *with the hearty solemnity of a Glee Club*:
   Lo! black as pitch
   The heavens are heavy with menace!
   The Men, whistling, howling and moaning, make storm 'effects'.

JENNY, BILL *bawling out*:
   Our ship is not a silk settee!
   Stormy the night and rampant the sea!
   O deck so shaky! O dark so quick!
   O S-O-S! Six of us three are sick!

MEN:
   Death now is nigh!
   Now black as pitch the sky . . .

JENNY *clinging anxiously to the 'mast'*: It might be best to sing
   'Stormy the Night' to keep up our courage.

BILL: 'Stormy the Night' is a wonderful tonic when your
courage begins to get shaky.

JIM: Then we'd better sing it at once.

JENNY, JIM, BILL:

Stormy the night and the white-caps high
'Courage', the Captain said:
Hark! like his echo the ship-bell rings –
Lo! there's a reef ahead!

JENNY: Go faster but go cautiously. Under no circumstances
sail against the wind or try out anything new.

MEN:

Listen
Hear how the wind in the rigging moans.
Look now
See where the heavens are pitch-black with menace!

BILL: Shouldn't we lash ourselves to the mast if the violence
of the storm increases?

JIM:

No, that is no menace, faithful shipmates
That's the black forest of Alaska.
Disembark.
We shall at last have peace.
He climbs down and calls:
Ahoy! Is that Alaska?

MOSES *slipping over to him*:

Come on, cough up the money!

JIM *deeply disappointed*:

No, it's Mahagonny.
The Men cluster around Jim, raising their glasses.

MEN:

Jimmy, old boy, you're a regular fellow
Standing us the drinks that make us mellow,
So with the same drinks we offer a toast:

Long life to Jimmy, the perfect host!

BEGBICK:

Well, it's time for paying – pet!

JIM:

Look, Lady Begbick, but what can I do now
If I'm not able to pay you yet?
My money, I notice, all is through now.

BEGBICK:

What! you don't want to pay now?

JENNY:

Jimmy, you must have a little more.
Why don't you go through your pockets again?

JIM:

I was telling you before . . .

MOSES:

What! the gentleman won't pay now?
What's that? No money? He really said it?
Do you realise what that means, my friend?

FATTY:

Sweetheart, this is your unhappy end.
All except Jenny and Bill have drawn away from Jim.

BEGBICK *to them*:

Couldn't *you* give him a little credit? *Bill walks away without
a word.* And you, Jenny?

JENNY:

Me?

BEGBICK:

You. Why not?

JENNY:

Don't make me laugh.
What will they ask a girl to do next?

BEGBICK:

Wouldn't you even consider putting up half?

JENNY:

No! If you have to have the precise text.

MOSES:

Put them on!

While Jim is being put in irons, Jenny comes downstage and walks up and down the apron singing:

JENNY:

Let me tell you what my mother called me –
A bad word – yessir, that's what.
She swore I would end on a morgue-slab
Or an even more unhealthy spot.
Well, things like that don't cost much to say,
But what *I* say is: Wait around and see!
The talk doesn't matter two hoots
For you won't make those things happen to me!
We're human, not brutes.
As you make your bed, so you lie on it:
The proverb is old but it's true.
So if someone must kick, why, that's my part
And another get kicked, that part's for you!

Have you heard yet what some guy told me?
'There's one thing can't be bought –
That's true love, the crown of existence.'
Also 'Give tomorrow no thought'.
Well, such things don't cost much to say
But what's mankind got to do with love
When each one gets older each day
And shorter grows the time we must make use of?
We're human, not brutes!
As you make your bed, so you lie on it:
The proverb is old but it's true.
So if someone must kick, why, that's my part

And another get kicked, that part's for you.

MOSES:

You'll observe this miserable wreck

Who ordered drinks and couldn't pay his check.

Why, there's gall in that to choke one!

What man's viler than a broke one?

Jim is taken out.

This is a capital offence!

A thousand pardons for the disturbance, gents.

All take their places again, drinking and playing billiards.

MEN:

Stay-at-homes do very well

Don't need daily twenty dollars;

Those who also marry tell

How they save a little extra:

So today they all are callers

At the Lord-and-Shepherd's second-class saloon;

They keep clean there in shirts and collars

Stamping in time with the music.

But they never see the moon.

They lean back slowly and put their feet up on the tables again.

Downstage men move along the apron and then go back to go off

upstage.

One means to eat all you are able;

Two, to change your loves about;

Three means the ring and gaming table;

Four, to drink until you pass out.

Moreover, better get it clear

That Don'ts are not permitted here!

17

Jim lies in irons. It is night.

JIM:
    If the sky must lighten
    Then a new goddam day begins.
    But the sky still is covered up in darkness.
    Let the dark
    Last forever
    Day must not
    Break at all.

    I'm still afraid they soon will be here.

    I'll lie and sink in roots below me
    When I hear them.
    They'll have to tear my roots up with me
    If they want me to go.
    Let the dark
    Last forever
    Day must not break at all.

    That's the kind of poker hand
    They dealt you;
    Play it out.
    What you lived of life
    Was good enough for you.
    What it brings now –
    That's the hand you're stuck with.

Surely the sky won't ever lose its darkness.
It begins to grow light.
It must not lighten.
There must be no sunrise.
That means a new goddam day begins.

18

Every city has its own notion of what is just, and Mahagonny's was no sillier than that of any other place

A courtroom in a tent. In the centre, a table and three chairs. Behind them rise tiers of benches on which the Public is sitting, reading newspapers, chewing gum and smoking. The set suggests an operating theatre. Begbick is in the judge's chair, Fatty in that of the defence attorney. On the prisoner's bench, to one side, sits a man. Moses, the prosecutor, is standing at the entrance.

MOSES:
   Have the folks here all paid their admissions?
   Three tickets still to go, at only five each!
   Two absolutely first-class tri-als –
   Five dollars buys a seat for both!
   Where could you find such a bargain?
   A measly fine to watch Justice in action!
   When no one else comes in, he resumes his place as prosecutor.
   First comes the case of Toby Higgins.

   The man on the prisoner's bench rises.
   He is charged with premeditated murder

Done to test a newly purchased revolver.
Never yet
Has there been a crime so fraught
With brutal baseness.
Toby Higgins, you have outraged
Every decent feeling known.
Yea, the naked soul of sorely wounded Righteousness
Cries out for its retribution.
I therefore must now as prosecutor move
Owing to the stubborn unrepentance this defendant –
This abyss of mean obscene corruption – still displays
That we let the Law take its course unhindered . . .
Hesitating:
And that he . . .
Under the circumstances . . .
Be acquitted!
During the 'prosecutor's' speech, a silent battle is taking place between Begbick and the Accused. By raising his finger, the Accused has indicated the amount of the bribe he is prepared to pay. In the same manner, Begbick raises her demands higher and higher. The pause at the end of Moses's speech marks the point when the Accused has raised his offer for the last time.
BEGBICK: Has the defence any point to raise?
FATTY: Who's the injured party here?
Silence.
BEGBICK: Since no injured party comes forward . . .
MEN *spectators*: Since dead men tell no tales . . .
BEGBICK: We by law have no course but acquitting him.
The Accused goes to join the spectators.
MOSES *reading*:
Second, the case of Jimmy Gallagher
For seduction, homicide, subversion and fraud.
Jim, handcuffed, is brought in by Bill.

JIM *before he takes his place on the prisoner's bench*:
  Billy, let me have a hundred dollars.
  It may help to make the court more friendly.

BILL:
  Jim, we're close as friends, you know:
  But with money, it's another matter.

JIM:
  Bill, you can't have forgotten
  About our time up in Alaska:
  Those seven winters of bitter weather
  When we felled timber, we two together.
  Please give me the dough.

BILL:
  I have never forgotten
  About our time up in Alaska:
  Those seven winters of bitter weather
  When we felled timber, we two together,
  And how hard we worked
  To make any money.
  That's why I simply can't
  Give you the money.

MOSES:
  The accused ordered rounds of whisky two times
  And broke a bar-rail, and did not pay.
  Never yet
  Has there been a crime so fraught
  With brutal baseness.
  Jimmy Gallagher, you've outraged
  Every decent feeling known.
  Yea, the naked soul of sorely wounded Righteousness
  Cries out for its retribution.
  I therefore must now as prosecutor move
  That we let the Law take its course unhindered.

During the prosecutor's speech, Jim does not respond to Begbick's finger-play. Begbick, Fatty and Moses exchange significant glances.

BEGBICK:

Now we'll proceed to itemise the varied crimes
Charged to you, Jimmy Gallagher!
That, barely off the boat, you did with forethought
Seduce here a girl, by name Jenny Jones
And made her do what you would
By means of your money.

FATTY: Who's the injured party here?

JENNY *coming forward*: Me. I am.

A murmur among the spectators.

BEGBICK:

That, while we waited the big typhoon
You did, in that hour of desperation
Persist in singing a cheerful song.

FATTY: Who's the injured party here?

MEN:

The injured party has not come forth.
Maybe there's no injured party here.
If there's no injured party at all
Then there might be some hope for you, Jimmy Gallagher!

MOSES *breaking in*:

But that very night the man
Before you now behaved worse
Than a typhoon ever could
Subverting all our city meant
By destroying concord and peace here!

MEN: Three cheers for Jimmy!

BILL *standing up among the spectators*:

But this untutored lumberjack from Alaska
Had a vision of happiness that very night
And gave the laws of life to Mahagonny.

Remember, they came from Jimmy.

MEN:

You must bring in acquittal then for Jimmy Gallagher
The lumberjack from Alaska!

BILL:

Jim, I'm glad to do this for you
For I think of old Alaska
Those seven winters of bitter weather
When we felled timber, we two together.

JIM:

Bill, what you've done here to help me
Takes me back once more to Alaska
To seven winters of bitter weather
When we felled timber, we two together.

MOSES *pounding the table*:

And remember the boxing-match
When your dear 'untutored lumberjack from Alaska' –
To win mere money his motive –
Drove his best friend to sudden and certain death.

BILL *jumping up*:

Yes, but who, august tribunal
Who's the party whose punch really killed him?

BEGBICK: Well then, who did kill the so-called Alaskawolf
Joe?

MOSES *after a pause*: That, your honour, is unknown to this
court.

BILL:

Of all those hanging around the ring that night
Not one was risking a bet
On a man who might give his life there
But the man who stands before you risking his!

MEN *alternately*:

The verdict must be guilty then for Jimmy Gallagher!

You must bring in acquittal then for Jimmy Gallagher!
Jimmy Gallagher, the lumberjack from Alaska!
Applause and hissing.

MOSES:

But now the crown of our charges comes:
Yourself, you ordered two rounds of whisky
And destroyed one bar-rail just to amuse yourself –
Then tell me why, yes, why, Jimmy Gallagher
You have failed to pay for consuming them.

JIM: Because I am broke.

MEN:

The man is broke.
He consumes what he can't pay for.
Down, down with Jimmy Gallagher!
Take him away!

BEGBICK, FATTY AND MOSES: Who claim to be injured
parties here?
Begbick, Fatty and Moses rise.

MEN:

Three injured parties have shown themselves.
They are the true injured parties then.

FATTY: Your verdict, august tribunal!

BEGBICK: In view of the unpropitious economic situation
the tribunal will make itself allowances for mitigating circumstances. Jimmy Gallagher, you are sentenced . . .

MOSES: For conniving at the murder of a friend . . .

BEGBICK: To three days arrest.

MOSES: For destroying the concord and peace here . . .

BEGBICK: A year's loss of civil rights.

MOSES: For the seduction of a girl by name of Jenny . . .

BEGBICK: To four years in prison.

MOSES: And for singing forbidden songs during the big
typhoon . . .

BEGBICK:

    To ten years hard labour.

    But for my two rounds of whisky unpaid for

    And my one bar-rail as well unpaid for

    You by law must be sentenced to death in the electric chair.

BEGBICK, FATTY AND MOSES:

    For the penniless man

    Is the worst kind of criminal

    Beyond both pity and pardon.

    Wild applause.

19

Execution of Jimmy Gallagher. Many of you, perhaps, will be shocked at what you are about to see. But, Ladies and Gentlemen, ask yourselves this question: 'Would *I* have paid Jimmy Gallagher's debts?' Would you? Are you sure?

On the backcloth is projected a general view of Mahagonny bathed in a peaceful light. Many people are standing about in groups. On the right, an electric chair is being erected. Jim enters accompanied by Moses, Jenny and Bill. The Men remove their hats.

MOSES:

    Good day!

    Didn't you hear me? I said Good day.

JIM *laconically*:

    Hi.

MOSES:

If you've any worldly business to wind up, you'd better do
  it now
For the gentlemen who are anxious to witness your
  departure
Have no interest in your private affairs.

JIM:

Darling Jenny
My time has come.
The days I have spent with you
Have been happy days
And happy too
Is the ending.

JENNY:

Darling Jimmy
I also have had my golden summertime
With you
And I dread what
Will become of me now.

JIM:

Jenny dear
My sort are not so hard to find.

JENNY:

That isn't true.
I know what is gone is gone forever.

JIM:

Why, you're wearing a white dress
Just like a widow.

JENNY:

Yes. Your widow is what I am
Jimmy, and I shan't forget you
When I'm just one
Of the girls again.

JIM:

Kiss me, Jenny.

JENNY:

Kiss me, Jimmy.

JIM:

Don't be sore at me.

JENNY:

Why should I be?

JIM:

Kiss me, Jenny.

JENNY:

Kiss me, Jimmy.

JIMMY:

And now I leave you, my dear

To my best and last friend, Billy

Who's the only one left

Of the four men who came

From the woods of cold Alaska.

BILL *taking Jenny in his arms*:

So long, Jim.

JIM:

So long, Bill.

They turn towards the place of execution.

A GROUP OF MEN *tell one another as they pass by*:

One means to eat all you are able;

Two, to change your loves about;

Three means the ring and gaming table;

Four, to drink until you pass out.

Jim stops and watches them.

MOSES:

Have you anything more to say?

JIM: So you really mean to execute me?

BEGBICK: Why not? It's customary.

JIM: You don't seem to know that there's a God.

BEGBICK: A what?

JIM: A God.

BEGBICK: Oh, *Him*! Don't be silly. Didn't you ever see the play: *God Comes to Mahagonny*? We'll put it on now for you, if you like; and you shall have the best seat in the house. Just sit yourself in this chair.

Four men and Jenny Jones appear before Jimmy Gallagher and act the play of God in Mahagonny.

THE FOUR MEN:

One morning when the sky was grey
During the whisky
God came to Mahagonny:
During the whisky
We recognised God in Mahagonny.

Moses, who plays the role of God, detaches himself from the others, steps forward and covers his face with his hat.

MOSES:

Insatiable sponges
Lapping up my harvest year by year!
Little have you reckoned with your Maker!
Are you ready now when I appear?

JENNY:

Saw what they were, the people of Mahagonny:
Yes, answered the people of Mahagonny.

THE FOUR:

One morning when the sky was grey
During the whisky
God came to Mahagonny:
During the whisky
We recognised God in Mahagonny.

MOSES:

Did you laugh on Friday evening?

I saw Mary Weeman swimming by
Like a salted cod-fish in the salt sea:
Mary never will again be dry.

JENNY:

Saw what they were, the people of Mahagonny:
Yes, answered the people of Mahagonny.

THE FOUR *behaving as though they hadn't heard anything*:

One morning when the sky was grey
During the whisky
God came to Mahagonny:
During the whisky
We recognised God in Mahagonny.

MOSES:

Whose is this ammunition?
Shot her, did you, shot my deaconess?
Are my thrones for brutes of your condition?
Is it drunken loafers I must bless?

JENNY:

Saw what they were, the people of Mahagonny:
Yes, answered the people of Mahagonny.

THE FOUR:

One morning when the sky was grey
During the whisky
God came to Mahagonny:
During the whisky
We recognised God in Mahagonny.

MOSES:

Down with all into hell-fire
Stuff your Henry Clays into your pack
Off with all of you to Hell, you scoundrels
Wriggle in the Devil's crowded sack!

JENNY:

Saw what they were, the people of Mahagonny:

No, answered the people of Mahagonny.

THE FOUR:

One morning when the sky was grey
During the whisky
You came to Mahagonny
During the whisky
Got going in Mahagonny.

But we won't budge a foot now!
We'll go on strike. We will never
Let you drag us off to Hell forever
For we *are* in Hell and always have been.

JENNY *through a megaphone*:

Saw God, they did, the people of Mahagonny:
No, answered the people of Mahagonny.

JIM:

Now I see it. When I came to this city, hoping that my money would buy me joy, my doom was already sealed. Here I sit now and have had just nothing. I was the one who said 'Everyone must carve himself a slice of meat, using any available knife'. But the meat had gone bad. The joy I bought was no joy; the freedom they sold me was no freedom. I ate and remained unsatisfied; I drank and became all the thirstier. Give me a glass of water.

MOSES *putting the helmet over his head*:

Ready!

20

And amid increasing confusion, inflation and universal mutual hostility those who had not yet been killed demonstrated for their ideals during the last weeks of Suckerville – having learnt nothing

Mahagonny is seen in flames on the screens in the background. Then groups of demonstrators begin appearing; they interweave and confront one another, continuing right up to the end.

First group. Begbick, Fatty the Bookie, Trinity Moses and supporters. The inscriptions on the first group's signs read:
'FOR THE INFLATION'
'FOR THE BATTLE OF ALL AGAINST ALL'
'FOR THE CHAOTIC STATE OF OUR CITIES'
'FOR THE PROLONGATION OF THE GOLDEN AGE'
FIRST GROUP:
For this splendid Mahagonny
Has it all, if you have the money.
Then all is available
Because all is for sale
And there is nothing that one cannot buy.
The inscriptions on the second group's signs read:
'FOR PROPERTY'
'FOR THE EXPROPRIATION OF OTHERS'
'FOR THE JUST DIVISION OF SPIRITUAL GOODS'
'FOR THE UNJUST DIVISION OF TEMPORAL GOODS'
'FOR LOVE'
'FOR THE BUYING AND SELLING OF LOVE'

'FOR THE NATURAL DISORDER OF THINGS'
'FOR THE PROLONGATION OF THE GOLDEN AGE'
SECOND GROUP:
   We need no raging hurricane
   We need no bolt from the blue:
   There's no havoc they might have done
   That we cannot better do.
The inscriptions on the third group's signs read:
'FOR FREEDOM FOR THE RICH'
'FOR VALOUR AGAINST THE DEFENCELESS'
'FOR HONOUR AMONG MURDERERS'
'FOR GREATNESS OF SQUALOR'
'FOR IMMORTALITY OF UNDERHANDEDNESS'
'FOR THE CONTINUATION OF THE GOLDEN AGE'
THIRD GROUP:
   As you make your bed so you lie on it
   The bed can be old or brand-new:
   So if someone must kick, that is my part
   And another get kicked, that part's for you.
FIRST GROUP *returning with its signs*:
   Why, though, did we need a Mahagonny?
   Because this world is a foul one
   With neither charity
   Nor peace nor concord
   Because there's nothing
   To build any trust upon.
FOURTH GROUP *of girls bearing Jim Gallagher's watch, revolver
and cheque book on a linen cushion, also his shirt on a pole*:
   Oh, Moon of Alabama
   We now must say good-bye.
   We've lost our good old mama
   And must have dollars
   Oh, you know why.

Fifth group carrying Jim Gallagher's body. Immediately following
them a sign with the inscription:
'FOR JUSTICE'

FIFTH GROUP:

You can bring vinegar – to him
You can wipe his forehead – for him
You can find surgical forceps
You can pull the tongue from his gullet
Can't do anything to help a dead man.

Sixth group with a small sign:
'FOR BRUTE STUPIDITY'

SIXTH GROUP:

You can talk good sense – to him
You can bawl oaths – at him
You can just leave him lying
You can take care – of him
Can't give orders, can't lay down any law to a dead man.
You can put coins in his hand – for him
You can dig a hole – by him
You can stuff that hole – with him
You can heap a shovelful – on him
Can't do anything to help a dead man.

Seventh group with an enormous placard:
'FOR THE CONTINUATION OF THE GOLDEN AGE'

SEVENTH GROUP:

You can talk about the glory of his heyday
You can also forget his old days completely
Can't do anything to help a dead man.
Unending groups in constant motion.

ALL GROUPS:

Can't help him or you or me or no one.

The Seven Deadly Sins of the Petty Bourgeoisie

Ballet

Collaborator: K. WEILL

Translators: W. H. AUDEN and CHESTER KALLMAN

The Seven Deadly Sins of the Petty Bourgeoisie

SLOTH
  in doing a wrong
PRIDE
  in one's best characteristic (Incorruptibility)
WRATH
  at mean behaviour
GLUTTONY
  (Satedness, Self-devouring)
LUST
  (Selfless love)
AVARICE
  in pillage and deception
ENVY
  of the fortunate

This ballet is meant to represent the journey of two sisters from the southern states who hope to get enough money to buy a small house for themselves and their family. Both are called Annie. One of the two Annie is the manager, the other the artiste; one (Annie I) is the saleslady, the other (Annie II) the article sold. On the stage stands a small board showing the course of their travels through seven cities; Annie I stands before it with a small pointer. Likewise on the stage is the continually fluctuating market on which Annie I launches her sister. At the end of each scene showing how the seven deadly sins can be avoided Annie II returns to Annie I, with their family on stage and the little house which they have acquired by avoiding the seven deadly sins in the background.

Prologue

ANNIE I:
> So my sister and I left Louisiana
> Where the moon on the Mississippi is a-shining ever
> Like you've heard about in the songs of Dixie.
> We look forward to our home-coming –
> And the sooner the better.

ANNIE II:
> And the sooner the better.

ANNIE I:
> It's a month already since we started
> For the great big cities where you go to make money.
> In seven years our fortune will be made
> And then we can go back.

ANNIE II:
> In six would be nicer.

ANNIE I:

Our mum and dad and both our brothers wait in old
    Louisiana
And we'll send them all our money as we make it
For all the money's got to go to build a little home
Down by the Mississippi in Louisiana.
Right, Annie?

ANNIE II:

Right, Annie.

ANNIE I:

She's the one with the looks, I'm realistic;
She's just a little mad, my head is on straight.
You may think that you can see two people
But in fact you see only one
And both of us are Annie:
Together we've but a single past, a single future
And one heart and savings-account;
And we only do what is best for each other.
Right, Annie?

ANNIE II:

Right, Annie.

I

Sloth

This is the first city on their journey, and the sisters get their first money by a trick. As they stroll through the city park they are on the lookout for married couples. Annie II hurls herself on a man as if she knew him; she flings her arms round him, reproaches him etc., in short reduces him to embarrassment while Annie I tries to restrain her. While Annie I is extracting money from the man for having got rid of

*her sister, Annie II suddenly falls on the wife and threatens her with
her parasol. They swiftly perform this trick a number of times. After
that however Annie I tries to blackmail a man she has enticed away
from his wife, on the assumption that her sister will meanwhile have
importuned the wife. She is appalled to see that her sister is sitting
dozing on a bench instead of getting on with the job. She is forced to
wake her up and set her to work.*

FAMILY:

Will she now? . . . will our Annie pull herself together?
    Lazy Bones are for the Devil's stock-pot –
For she was always quite a one for an arm-chair;
    Lazy Bones are for the Devil's stock-pot –
Unless you came and hauled her off the mattress
    Lazy Bones are for the Devil's stock-pot –
The lazy slug would lie abed all morning.
    Lazy Bones are for the Devil's stock-pot –
Otherwise, Annie was, we must admit, a most respectful
       child,
    Lazy Bones are for the Devil's stock-pot –
Did what she was told and showed affection for her
       parents.
    Lazy Bones are for the Devil's stock-pot –
This is what we told her when she left home:
    Lazy Bones are for the Devil's stock-pot –
'Think of us, and mind you keep your nose down to the
       grind-stone.'

    O Lord, look down upon our daughter
    Show her the way that leads the Good to Thy reward
In all her doings prevent her and comfort her
    Incline her heart to observe all Thy commandments
    That her works on earth may prosper.

2

Pride

A dirty little cabaret. Annie II enters to the applause of 4–5 customers whose frightful appearance greatly alarms her. Though poorly clad she dances in a most unusual way, puts her soul into it and is badly received. The customers are infinitely bored; they yawn like sharks (their masks portraying horrible teeth in preternaturally large mouths), hurl things on to the stage and manage to bring the one lamp crashing down. Annie II goes on dancing, utterly wrapped up in her art until removed from the stage by the proprietor. He sends on another dancer, a fat old frump who shows Annie how to set about winning applause in his establishment. The old frump dances in a vulgar sexy way and is vastly applauded. Annie refuses to dance like that. But Annie I, who has been standing beside the stage where she was the only one to applaud her sister and wept to see her lack of success, now gets her to dance in the required manner. As her skirt is too long, Annie I rips it off and sends her back on stage to be shown how to dance by the frump, pulling her skirts up higher and higher to the applause of the audience. And it is she who leads her sister back to the small board to be comforted.

ANNIE I:
   So we
   Saved up
   Bought ourselves an outfit:
   Nighties
   Nylons
   Beautiful dresses:
   Soon we
   Found a

Job that was going
A job as dancer in a cabaret
A job in Memphis, the second big town we came to
Oh how hard it was for Annie!
Beautiful clothes can make a good girl particular –
When the drinking tigress meets herself in the pool
She's apt to become a menace.
She began talking about art, of all things
About the Art, if you please, of Cabaret
In Memphis, the second big town we came to.

It wasn't art that sort of people came for
That sort of people came for something else;
And when a man has paid for his evening
He expects a good show in return.
So if you cover up your bosom and thighs like you had a
    rash
Don't be surprised to see them yawning.

So I told my art-loving sister Annie:
'Leave your pride to those who can well afford it.
Do what you are asked to do and not what you want
For that isn't what is wanted.'
Oh but
I had
Trouble, I can tell you
With her
Fancy
Pig-headed notions.
Many
Nights I
Sat by her bedside
Holding her hand and saying this:

'Think of our home in Louisiana.'

FAMILY:

O Lord, look down upon our daughter
Show her the way that leads the Good to Thy reward.
Who fights the Good Fight and all Self subdues
Wins the Palm, gains the Crown.

We're at a standstill! What she's been sending
It's not any money a man can build a home with.
She's as giddy as a cyclone!
All the profits go for her pleasure!
And we're at a standstill, for what she's been sending
Is not any money a man can build a home with.
Won't she settle down to business?
Won't she ever learn to save something?
For what the featherbrain is sending
Is not any kind of money
A man can build a little home with.

3

Wrath

A film is being made in which Annie is an extra. The star, a Douglas Fairbanks type, rides his horse over a basket of flowers. The horse is clumsy, so he beats it. It falls and is unable to get up despite the blanket they put beneath it and the sugar they put before it. So he beats it again. But at that point the little extra steps forward, takes the whip from his hand and, in her wrath, beats him instead. She is promptly dismissed. However, her sister rounds on her and per-

suades her to come back, go on bended knee to the star and kiss his
hand; upon which he once again recommends her to the director.

ANNIE I:

 We're making progress. We have come to Los Angeles
 And every door is open here to welcome extras.
 We only need a bit of practice avoiding possible faux pas
 And what can stop us going straight to the top then?

FAMILY:

 O Lord, look down upon our daughter
 Show her the way that leads the Good to Thy reward.

ANNIE I:

 If you take offence at Injustice
 Mister Big will show he's offended;
 If a curse or a blow can enrage you so
 Your usefulness here is ended.

 Then mind what the Good Book tells us
 When it says: 'Resist not Evil.'
 Unforgiving Anger
 Is from the Devil.

 It took time to teach my sister wrath wouldn't do
 In Los Angeles the third big town we came to
 Where her open disapproval of injustice
 Was so widely disapproved.
 I forever told her: 'Practise self-control, Annie
 For you know how much it costs you if you don't.'
 And she saw my point and answered:

ANNIE II:

 Yes I know, Annie.

4
Gluttony

Annie has herself become a star. Having signed a contract forbidding her to put on weight, she must not eat. One day she steals an apple and furtively eats it; and when she is weighed and found to weigh one gramme more, the impresario tears his hair out. From then on her eating is supervised by her sister. Two flunkeys with revolvers serve her food, and all she is allowed to take from the dish is a little miniature bottle.

FAMILY:
We've gotten word from Philadelphia:
Annie's doing well, she's making money.
Her contract has been signed to do a solo turn.
It forbids her ever eating when or what she likes to eat.
Those are hard terms for little Annie:
Who has always been very greedy.
Oh if only she doesn't break her contract –
There's no market for hippos in Philadelphia.
Every single day they weigh her.
Gaining half an ounce means trouble.
They have principles to stand by:
It's a hundred-and-eighteen that you were signed for –
Only for the weight agreed we pay!
Gaining half an ounce means trouble
More than that would mean disaster!

But our Annie isn't all that stupid
And she knows a contract is a contract
So she'll reason: After all

You still can eat like little Annie
In Louisiana –
Crabmeat! Porkchops! Sweet-corn! Chicken!
And those golden biscuits spread with honey!
Spare your home in old Louisiana!
Think! – It's growing! More and more it needs you!
Therefore curb your craving! Gluttons will be punished!

5

Lust

Annie now has an admirer who is extremely rich, loves her and brings her jewels and clothes; likewise a lover whom she in turn loves and who takes the jewels off her. Annie I reproaches her and persuades her to leave Fernando and be faithful to Edward. But one day Annie II passes a café where Annie I is sitting with Fernando, who is paying court to her (though to no effect). Thereupon Annie II assaults Annie I and they roll about in the street wrestling under the eyes of Fernando and his friends, together with a horde of street children and bystanders. The children point out her valuable bottom, and Edward runs away in horror. Then Annie I reproaches her sister and, after a touching parting from Fernando, sends her back to Edward.

ANNIE I:
Then we met a wealthy man in Boston
And he paid her a lot because he loved her.
But I had to keep a watch on Annie
Who was too loving, and she loved another;
And she paid him a lot
Because she loved him.

So I said: 'Cheat the man who protects you
And you've lost half your value then:
He may pay once although he suspects you
But he won't pay time and time again.

You can have your fun with money
When you've no provider you must face;
But for girls like us, it's not funny
If we ever even once forget our place.'

'Don't try to sit between two stools,' I told her.
Then I went to visit her friend
And said: 'If you're kind, you won't hold her,
For this love will be your sweetheart's bitter end.'

Girls can have their fun with money
When the money is their own to give;
But for girls like us, it's not funny
If we even once forget the way we live.'

Then I'd meet him as bad luck would have it.
There was nothing going on. Naturally!
Until Annie found out and, worse luck
Blamed the whole affair on me.

FAMILY:
O Lord, look down upon our daughter
Show her the way that leads the Good to Thy reward
Incline her heart to observe all Thy commandments
That her works on earth may prosper.

ANNIE I:
Now she shows off her little round white fanny
Worth twice a little Texas Motel
And for nothing the poolroom can stare at Annie

As though she'd nothing to sell.
That's why most girls don't get rich, for
They go wrong when they forget their place:
You're not free to buy what you itch for
When you've got a good provider you must face.

FAMILY:

Who fights the Good Fight and all Self subdues
Will gain her renown.

ANNIE I:

It wasn't easy putting *that* in order:
Saying good-bye to young Fernando
Then back to Edward to apologise
Then the endless nights I heard my sister
Sobbing like a baby and repeating;

ANNIE II:

It's right like this, Annie, but so hard!

6

Avarice

Shortly afterwards Edward shoots himself, having been ruined by Annie. Then the newspapers print flattering reports about her, with the effect that the readers doff their hats to her respectfully and immediately follow her, newspaper in hand, in the hope of being ruined too. Soon after that another young man flings himself out of a window after Annie has left him penniless; then her sister intervenes and saves yet another one from hanging himself, by taking his money back from Annie II and returning it to him. She does this because

*people are starting to shun her sister, who has got a bad name on
account of her avarice.*

FAMILY:
>   Annie, so the paper says
>   Is now set up in Baltimore:
>   Lots of folk seem to be
>   Shooting themselves for her.
>   She must be doing all right
>   And raking it in,
>   To get in the news like that!
>   Well, so far, so good; to be talked about helps
>   A young girl up the ladder.
>   Let her beware of overdoing it!
>   Folk shy away from a girl
>   Who's said to be mean.
>
>   Folk give a wide wide berth
>   To those who grab all they can get
>   Point unfriendly fingers at
>   One whose greed goes beyond all bounds.
>   In the measure you give
>   You will surely be given
>   And as you do, so
>   Will you be done by:
>   Fair is fair.
>   All must keep this law.
>
>   We sincerely hope our smart little Annie
>   Also has common sense
>   And will let them keep a shirt or two
>   When she lets them go for good.
>
>   Shameless hoarders earn themselves a bad name.

7
Envy

Once again we see Annie traversing the big city and glimpsing other Annies as she goes – all the other dancers being masked to look like Annie – who indulge in idleness etc. etc., thereby committing with impunity all those deadly sins that have been forbidden her. A ballet represents the theme THE LAST SHALL BE FIRST *thus: As the other Annies proudly walk around in the light, Annie II laboriously drags herself in, bent double. But then her apotheosis begins and she walks with increasing pride, finally triumphing as the other Annies crumple, abashed, and are forced to make way for her.*

ANNIE:
  And the last big town we came to was San Francisco.
  Life, there, was fine, only Annie felt so tired
  And grew envious of others:
  Of those who pass the time at their ease and in comfort
  Those too proud to be bought –
  Of those whose wrath is kindled by injustice
  Those who act upon their impulses happily
  Lovers true to their loved ones
  And those who take what they need without shame.
  Whereupon I told my poor tired sister
  When I saw how much she envied them:

  'Sister, from birth we may write our own story
  And anything we choose we are permitted to do
  But the proud and insolent who strut in their glory –
  Little they guess
  Little they guess
  Little they guess the fate they're swaggering to.

'Sister, be strong! You must learn to say No to
The joys of this world, for this world is a snare;
Only the fools in this world will let go, who
Don't care a damn
Don't care a damn –
Don't-care-a-damn will be made to care.

'Don't let the flesh and its longings get you.
Remember the price that a lover must pay
And say to yourself when temptations beset you –
What is the use?
What is the use?
Beauty will perish and youth pass away.

'Sister, you know, when our life here is over
Those who were good go to bliss unalloyed
Those who were bad are rejected forever
Gnashing their teeth
Gnashing their teeth
Gnashing their teeth in a gibbering void!

FAMILY:
Who fights the Good Fight and all Self subdues
Wins the Palm, gains the Crown.

Epilogue

ANNIE I:

Now we're coming back to you, Louisiana
Where the moon on the Mississippi is a-shining ever.
Seven years we're been away in the big towns
Where one goes to make money;
And now our fortune's made, and now you're there
Little home in old Louisiana.
We're coming back to you
Out little home down by
The Mississippi in
Louisiana. . . .
Right, Annie.

ANNIE II:

Right, Annie.

Notes and Variants

Text by Brecht

OPERA –

Our existing opera is a culinary opera. It was a means of pleasure long before it turned into merchandise. It furthers pleasure even where it requires, or promotes, a certain degree of education, for the education in question is an education of taste. To every object it adopts a hedonistic approach. It 'experiences', and it ranks as an 'experience'.

Why is *Mahagonny* an opera? Because its basic attitude is that of an opera: that is to say culinary. Does *Mahagonny* adopt a hedonistic approach? It does. Is *Mahagonny* an experience? It is an experience. For – *Mahagonny* is a piece of fun.

The opera Mahagonny *pays conscious tribute to the irrationality of the operatic form*. The irrationality of opera lies in the fact that rational elements are employed, solid reality is aimed at, but at the same time it is all washed out by the music. A dying man is real. If at the same time he sings we are translated to the sphere of the irrational. (If the audience sang at the sight of him the case would be different.)

The more unclear and unreal the music can make the reality – though there is of course a third, highly complex and in itself quite real element which can have quite real effects but is utterly remote from the reality of which it treats – the more pleasurable the whole process becomes: the pleasure grows in proportion to the degree of unreality.

The concept of opera – far be it from us to profane it – leads in *Mahagonny*'s case to all the rest. The intention was that a certain unreality, irrationality and lack of seriousness should be introduced at the right moment, and wash itself out altogether.[1] The irrationality which enters thus only fits the point where it enters.

[1] These narrow limitations do not prevent the introduction of an element of

Such an approach is purely hedonistic.

As for the content of this opera, *its content is pleasure*. Fun, in other words, not only as form but as object. At least, enjoyment was meant to be the object of the inquiry even if the inquiry was intended to be an object of enjoyment. Enjoyment appears here in its current historical role: as merchandise.[2]

It is undeniable that this content is bound at present to have a provocative effect. In the thirteenth section, for instance, where the glutton stuffs himself to death, it is provocative because hunger is the rule. Although we never even hinted that others were going hungry while he stuffed, the effect was provocative. Not everyone who is in a position to stuff himself dies of it, yet many are dying of hunger because he dies from stuffing himself. His pleasure is provocative because it implies so much.[3] Opera as a means of pleasure is generally provocative in contexts like this today. Not of course so far as the handful of opera-goers are concerned. In its power to provoke we can see reality reintroduced. *Mahagonny* may not taste all that good; it may even (thanks to guilty conscience) make a point of not doing so; but it is culinary through and through.

Mahagonny is nothing more or less than an opera.

---

instruction and directness or the basing of the whole arrangement on gests. The eye that reduces everything to its gestic aspect is morality. I.e. the depiction of mores. But from a subjective point of view . . .

> Let's have another drink
> Then we won't go home tonight
> Then we'll have another drink
> Then we'll have a break.

The people who sing like this are subjective moralists. They are describing themselves.

[2] Romanticism likewise is merchandise. It figures only as content, not as form.

[3] 'A dignified gentleman with an empurpled face had fished out a bunch of keys and was making a piercing demonstration against the Epic Theatre. His wife stood by him in this decisive moment. She stuck two fingers in her mouth, screwed up her eyes and blew out her cheeks. Her whistle made more noise than the key of his cash-box.' (Alfred Polgar, describing the Leipzig première of *Mahagonny*.)

– WITH INNOVATIONS!

When the epic theatre's methods begin to penetrate the opera the first result is a radical *separation of the elements*. The great struggle for supremacy between words, music and production – which always brings up the question 'which is the pretext for what?': is the music the pretext for the events on the stage, or are these the pretext for the music? etc. – can simply be bypassed by radically separating the elements. So long as the expression 'Gesamtkunstwerk' [or 'integrated work of art'] means that the integration is a macédoine, so long as the arts are supposed to be 'fused' together, the various elements will all be equally degraded and each will act as a mere 'feed' to the rest. The process of fusion extends to the spectator, who gets thrown into the melting pot too and becomes a passive (suffering) part of the total work of art. Witchcraft of this sort must of course be fought against. Whatever is intended to produce hypnosis, or is likely to induce improper intoxication, or creates fog, has got to be given up.

Words, music and setting must become more independent of one another.

(a) Music

For the music, the change of emphasis proved to be as follows:

Dramatic Opera	Epic Opera
The music dishes up	The music communicates
Music which heightens the text	Music which sets forth the text
Music which proclaims the text	Music which takes the text for granted
Music which illustrates	Which takes up a position
Music which depicts the psychological situation	Which gives the attitude

Music plays the chief part in our thesis.[4]

---

[4] The large number of craftsmen in the average opera orchestra allows of nothing but associative music (one flood of sound leading to another), and so the orchestral apparatus needs to be cut down to thirty specialists or less. The singer becomes a reporter, whose private feelings must remain a private affair.

(b) Text

We had to make something instructive and direct of our piece of fun if it was not to be merely irrational. The form that suggested itself was that of the moral tableau. The tableau is depicted by the characters in the play. The text had to be neither moralising nor sentimental, but to put morality and sentimentality on view. The spoken word was no more important than the written word (of the titles). Reading seems to encourage the audience to adopt the most relaxed attitude towards the work.

(c) Image

Showing independent works of art as part of a theatrical performance is a new departure. Neher's projections adopt an attitude towards the events on the stage; as when the real glutton sits in front of the glutton whom Neher has drawn. Each scene repeats in fluid form what is fixed in the image. These projections of Neher's are quite as much an independent component of the opera as are Weill's music and the text. They provide its visual aids.

Of course such innovations also demand a new attitude on the part of the audiences who frequent opera houses.

[. . .]

Perhaps *Mahagonny* is as culinary as ever – just as culinary as an opera ought to be – but one of its functions is to change society; it brings the culinary principle under discussion, it attacks the society that needs operas of such a sort; it still perches happily on the old limb, perhaps, but at least it has started (out of absent-mindedness or bad conscience) to saw it through. . . . And here you have the effect of the innovations and the song they sing.

Real innovations attack the roots.

[From 'Anmerkungen zur Oper "Aufstieg und Fall der Stadt Mahagonny" ' in GW *Schriften zum Theater*, p. 1004, originally published over the names of Brecht and (Peter) Suhrkamp in *Versuche 2*, 1931. These notes, which are given complete in *Brecht on Theatre* under the title 'The Modern Theatre is the

Epic Theatre', have here been shorn of those passages which are not primarily relevant to the present work. This has meant the omission of all section 1, the long table contrasting epic and dramatic theatre in section 3, all but the last two paragraphs of section 4 and the whole of section 5. The full essay is perhaps the most important pre-1933 statement of Brecht's ideas about the theatre in general.]

Notes by Weill and Neher

NOTES TO MY OPERA *Mahagonny*
by Kurt Weill

When Brecht and I first met in spring 1927 we were discussing the potentialities of opera, when the word 'Mahagonny' was mentioned and with it the notion of a 'paradise city'. The idea instantly seized me, and with a view to developing it and trying out the musical style I had in mind I set the five 'Mahagonny Songs' from Brecht's *Devotions for the Home*, combining them in a small-scale dramatic form to make a 'Songspiel' which was performed at Baden-Baden that summer. This Baden-Baden *Mahagonny* was thus nothing but a stylistic exercise for the opera proper, which had already been started and was taken up again as soon as the style had been tested. Brecht and I worked on its libretto for almost a year. The score was completed in November 1929.

The 'Song' form established in the Baden-Baden piece, and carried on in such subsequent works as *The Threepenny Opera*, the *Berlin Requiem* and *Happy End*, was of course inadequate for a full-length opera; it needed to be supplemented by other, larger-scale forms. None the less the simple ballad style had to be maintained.

The content of this opera is the history of a city: its foundation, its early crises, followed by the decisive turning-point in its evolution, its golden age and its decline. These constitute 'moral tableaux for the present day', projected on a large surface. It was a choice which allowed us to use the purest form of epic theatre, which is likewise the purest form of musical theatre. They make a sequence of twenty-one self-contained musical forms, each being a self-contained scene and each introduced by an inscription in narrative form. The music therefore no longer furthers the plot but only starts up once a situation has been arrived at. The libretto accordingly was arranged from the outset so as to represent a linear sequence of situations which add up to a dramatic form only in the course of their musically fixed dynamic succession.

['Anmerkungen zu meiner Oper "Mahagonny"', from Kurt Weill: *Ausgewählte Schriften*, ed. David Drew, Suhrkamp, Frankfurt 1975, p. 56. Reprinted from *Die Musik*, March 1930, Jg 22 Nr 6, p. 29.]

INTRODUCTION TO THE PROMPT-BOOK OF THE OPERA
Mahagonny
by Kurt Weill

The Threepenny Opera represented an attempt to revive the earliest form of musical theatre. The music in question does not further the plot; each entrance of the music, rather, amounts to an interruption of the plot. The epic form of theatre is a step-by-step juxtaposition of situations. This makes it the perfect form of musical theatre, since self-contained musical forms can only express situations, and the juxtaposition of situations according to musical criteria leads to that heightened form of musical theatre, an opera.

In *The Threepenny Opera* the plot had to be advanced in the intervals between the musical numbers. This led to something like a form of 'dialogue opera', a cross between opera and play.

With *The Rise and Fall of the City of Mahagonny* the material permits of *construction strictly according to the laws of music*. For the chronicle form here adopted is nothing but a 'juxtaposition of situations'. So each new situation in the history of the city of Mahagonny is introduced by an inscription which provides a bridge to the next scene in narrative form.

Two men and a woman, on the run from the constabulary, are stuck in a desolate area. They decide to found a city in which every man arriving from the gold coast can get his requirements satisfied. A 'paradise city' consequently springs up, whose inhabitants lead an idyllic life of contemplation. Sooner or later however the men from the gold coast become dissatisfied with it. Discontent sets in. Prices fall. During the night of the typhoon, while it is bearing down on the city, Jim Mahoney discovers the city's new law. It is 'Anything goes'. The typhoon veers away. Life goes on according to the new laws. The city blooms. People's requirements multiply – prices likewise. For anything goes: yes, but only so long as you can pay for it. Even Jim Mahoney gets condemned to death when he runs out of money. His execution sparks off a vast demonstration against the cost-of-living increases that herald the city's fall.

That is the story of the city of Mahagonny. It is conveyed in a loose form of juxtaposed 'twentieth-century moral tableaux'. It is a parable of modern life. The play's protagonist is the city. This springs from people's requirements, and it is these requirements that lead to its rise and fall. The individual phases of the city's history however are shown exclusively through their impact on people. For just as people's requirements influence the development of the city, so does the development of the city in turn influence people's attitudes. All the songs in this opera are accordingly expressions of the masses, even where it is a single representative of those masses that sings them. At the start the group of founders is set against the group of newcomers. At the end of Act 1 [i.e. after scene 11] the group supporting the new law is fighting the group of its opponents. The fate of the individual is only shown in passing, and then only when it stands for the fate of the city.

It would be wrong to look for any psychological or topical links except within the framework of this basic idea.

The name 'Mahagonny' signifies nothing except the notion of a city. Phonetic (sound) reasons determined its choice. The city's geographical location is not relevant.

It is not at all advisable to tilt the performance of this work in the direction of irony or the grotesque. The events are not symbolic but typical, and this entails the utmost economy of scenic means and individual expression on the part of the actors. The directing of the singers in their capacity as actors, the movements of the chorus, indeed the whole style of performance in this opera are all determined by the style of the music. This music is never in the least illustrative. It sets out to realise human attitudes in the various circumstances leading to the city's rise and fall. Human attitudes are already so embodied in the music that a simple, natural interpretation of the music will establish the right style for their portrayal. The actor accordingly can limit himself to the simplest and most natural gests.

In staging the opera it must always be borne in mind that one is dealing with *self-contained musical forms*. Hence it is important firmly to establish its purely musical development and to group the actors in such a way as to allow something close to a concert performance. Its style is neither naturalistic nor symbolic. It would be better described as 'real', since it shows life as represented in the sphere of art. Any exaggeration in the direction of emotion or ballet-like stylisation should be avoided.

Caspar Neher's projections are an essential part of the material going to make up the performance (and should accordingly be sent out to theatres along with the music). These projections make use of a painter's resources to provide an independent illustration of the events on stage. They supply visual aids to the history of the city, to be projected on a screen or between the individual scenes. The actor performs his scenes in front of the screen, and no more props are needed than are essential for him to clarify his performance. It is an opera that does not call for any use of complex stage machinery. The important thing is to have a few good projectors, together with an adroit arrangement of surfaces so that the pictures and still more the explanatory writing can be clearly understood from all parts of the house. The set needs to be so simple as to be equally well transferable from the theatre to any old platform. The solo scenes should be played as close to the audience as possible. It is therefore advisable not to sink the orchestra pit but to make it level with the stalls and build out a platform from the stage in such a way as to allow some scenes to be played in among the orchestra.

['Vorwort zum Regiebuch der Oper "Mahagonny" ', from Kurt Weill: *Ausgewählte Schriften*, ed. David Drew, Suhrkamp, Frankfurt 1975, p. 57, reprinted from *Anbruch*, Vienna, Jan 1930, Jg 12 Nr 1, p. 5. Drew cites *Anbruch*'s accompanying comment that Weill, Neher and Brecht were preparing a prompt-book for supplying to any theatre staging the work. This however seems not to have got beyond note form, as translated below, nor did Brecht in fact collaborate, his own 'Notes to the Opera' (p. 87ff) being independently written later. Weill wanted his Foreword to precede the notes that now follow.]

SUGGESTIONS FOR THE STAGE REALISATION OF THE
OPERA *The Rise and Fall of the City of Mahagonny*
by Kurt Weill and Caspar Neher

General

The background is formed by a big wooden (or canvas) screen which ideally should be capable of being pushed aside. Downstage a half-curtain 2.50 metres high running on a wire. Built out into the orchestra pit a semi-circular apron, size determined by the size of the orchestra, edged by a line of small lamps that can come into operation each time a scene is played on the apron. From its middle a gangway leads up on to the main stage. To start with it runs horizontally from the front of the apron, then it goes slantwise across the footlights on to the stage.

With respect to set and costumes, it is important to avoid any tendency to Wild West and Cowboy romanticism, as also any stressing of a typically American ambience.

Act 1

No. 1. The dialogue between Fatty and Moses to be sluggish and lazy and continually petering out.

No. 5. The side gangway is now a passenger gangway at the docks in Mahagonny and bears a sign 'To the boats'. Downstage left is a signpost not unlike a small gallows with a legible inscription saying 'To Mahagonny'. On the same side there is a big blackboard which can be chalked on. At the top it says 'Prices in the City of Mahagonny'.

The pictures of girls (p. 11) are rolled up like maps and hung on a cord in front of the list of prices. They are drawn in the Japanese manner. At the start of the scene the four men are on the apron. The whole scene is played partly on the apron, partly on the front part of the stage. [... At the end of the scene] Jim holds Jenny back and remains with her on the apron as the half-curtain closes behind them. [...]

No. 7. Half-curtain open. The lorry of scene 1 has been transformed into a kind of bar, inscribed 'The As-You-Like-It Tavern'. As Begbick gets more and more worked up the two men remain maliciously relaxed, which only adds to Begbick's anger. Their interpolations are accompanied by broad grins. [...]

No. 9. Half-curtain open. Again the As-You-Like-It Tavern. Minor improvements and developments however show that a certain amount of time has passed, during which the city has expanded. [...] At the beginning of the row [*He jumps to his feet*, p. 22], the male members of the chorus are relatively uninvolved. They merely express their resentment at having their rest disturbed. The more the row gets under way, the more scornful and threatening their attitude towards Jim ... till they become like a street riot. [...]

No. 10. All movement on stage is frozen. At figure 138 [of the musical introduction] projection number 10 (people fleeing). People fleeing rush across the front of the stage from left to right, with hand carts, luggage, women, children, animals; a wounded man is led past.... [Just before the entry of the chorus] the whole ensemble moves down to the front of the stage. [At its end] all disperse in different directions. A wind gets up, driving scraps of paper, leaves etc. before it.

The whole representation of the typhoon must take place without noises; there must be no storm or rain effects. When the chorus crashes [on its dispersal] Jenny, Begbick, Jake, Bill and Joe are left lying downstage motionless with their faces to the ground.

No. 11. Posters are stuck up on the wall saying 'It is prohibited...'.

Act 2

[...]

No. 13. Between numbers 12 and 13, projections 12, 13 and 14 are shown one after the other in total silence. They show the transition from a simple gold-prospectors' town to a modern city. Over each of them stand the words 'Do it' in big letters. [...]

No. 15. At figure 63 [i.e. at the end of their duet, p. 40] Joe and Jim pose in an attitude of friendship and are photographed by a press photographer. At [the Referee's entry] the combatants are weighed on a big decimal machine, Moses first, then Joe. [...]

No. 17. By the footlights stands a lantern. Against it, on a little platform, Jim stands in a wooden box that covers him from his neck to his knees. He is being put on public view. At first one or two people pass by him on their own during the short musical interludes. After that he is entirely alone. It is night. No light other than the lantern. [...]

Act 3

No. 18. A stand has been put up, consisting of three parts: one upstage centre, with left and right adjoining sections running slantwise downstage. It is so constructed that each row of seats is about 50 cm higher than the one in front. Right at the top behind the seats there is beer on tap. A plain wooden table stands in the centre at the bottom.

Moses's speech for the prosecution ('Never yet', p. 52) is delivered like a universally familiar song which a tedious formality demands; nobody listens to it; instead they are all following the bribery negotiations, and Moses himself is only interested in squeezing all he can out of the accused. During the murder case the spectators read the paper, smoke, drink beer. It is only with the opening of the case against Jimmy Gallagher that they start to show some interest [...]

No. 19 [20 in piano score]. [Initial stage direction as in our text, except that instead of the electric chair there is a makeshift gallows. As Jim sings 'Dreams have all one ending' (see editorial notes)] enter right a number of men, who quickly pass by

with a preoccupied air and disappear into the doorway of the
As-You-Like-It Tavern (now the height of elegance, complete
with revolving door etc.). [...]

After the words 'Is nothing but the grave' the half-curtain
closes. Behind it Moses can be heard giving the order 'Ready!'
(p. 62). Lights throughout the theatre flicker and suddenly
go out. Then the small lamps along the apron light up. Begbick
gets up, goes to the blackboard, crosses out the words 'Sold
Out' and substitutes '100 dollars'. She has some fresh whisky
bottles under her arm. Jenny and Bill enter through the half-
curtain. Bill and the murder-case man each give her a hundred-
dollar bill and take a bottle of whisky. Throughout the next
scene Begbick sits under the blackboard, saying nothing, but
clasping her two hundred-dollar notes.

Ditto [21 in piano score]. The [four] men start singing the song
of God in Mahagonny. [...] Moses appears through the half-
curtain wearing a long black coat, with his hat right down over
his eyes. The men are amazed that God should actually appear.
At first their answers are highly disconcerted, till in the end they
rebel with 'For we *are* in Hell and always have been!' (p. 62).
At the ensuing *Furioso* they break up the blackboard and the
chairs. Arming themselves with chair legs, planks and revolvers
they rush off through the half-curtain on to the main stage.

Finale [i.e. our no. 20]. [Initial stage direction as in our text,
except:] Each of the groups consists of about five to seven
people. [...] At the last line the wooden screen parts in the
middle, revealing a great number of groups, who advance in
between the leading columns. [...] They all start moving forward as if the entire demonstration, spreading right across the
stage, were proposing to march into the auditorium. When they
are almost down to the footlights the main curtain cuts them off.

['Vorschläge zur szenischen Aufführung der Oper "Aufstieg
und Fall der Stadt Mahagonny" ' in the Kurt Weill Archive.
Our translation is of extracts from a transcript kindly lent by
David Drew, shortened to eliminate points already in our text
or otherwise irrelevant. In the original the scene and page
references were all to the 1929 piano score; we have varied them
to refer to our text. The actual date of these 'Suggestions' is

November or December 1929, i.e. more than a year before the Leipzig première. Drew suggests that too many of them were then found to be unworkable for the collaborators to go ahead with their planned publication.]

Editorial Notes

Possibly the first of Brecht's writings about his mythical city was a fragmentary scene with two whores headed 'AUF NACH MAHA-GONNY', which seems to bear no relation at all to the subsequent opera. Already before leaving Bavaria however he had begun writing the 'Mahagonny Songs', of which three were included in his 1924 plan for his first collection of poems, the *Devotions for the Home*. There were four in all, each with a strongly American flavour (whisky, poker, Jack Dempsey, the moon of Alabama and so on), and in Berlin he added two more songs which his new collaborator Elisabeth Hauptmann actually wrote for him in English. These are almost the only tangible evidence of the kind of theme discussed by Brecht and Kurt Weill when they first met nearly three years later, shortly after the publication of the *Devotions*, which now included all six songs with Brecht's own tunes. What they at once envisaged, it seems, was a large-scale opera in which Mahagonny would emerge as a contemporary Sodom or Gomorrah. But the immediate task which presented itself in May 1927 was the provision of a small-scale 'scenic cantata' for the forthcoming Baden-Baden music festival, and they decided to base this on the Mahagonny Songs. Weill accordingly set Songs 1 to 3 (omitting the still unpublished no. 4) and the two English-language parodies, while Brecht wrote a new poem to serve as a finale under the title 'Aber dieses ganze Mahagonny'. The six songs were then alternated with orchestral interludes on the following pattern: Mahagonny Song no. 1 / Little March / Alabama Song / Vivace / Mahagonny Song no. 2 / Vivace assai / Benares Song / Sostenuto (Choral) / Mahagonny Song no. 3 / Vivace assai / Finale 'Aber dieses ganze Mahagonny'. There was no dialogue, but the characters were given suitably Anglo-Saxon names: Jessie, Bessie, Charlie, Billy, Bobby and Jimmy. This was the work performed on 17 July, after which it was shelved for the next thirty years.

A 'first sketch' for the opera, published in the magazine *Das neue Forum* in 1957/58, would appear to list the texts for Caspar Neher's projected scene titles in the Songspiel, as the Baden-Baden version was termed. They run: '1. The great cities in our day are full of people who do not like it there. 2. So get away to Mahagonny, the gold town situated on the shores of consolation far from the rush of the world. 3. Here in Mahagonny life is lovely. 4. But even in Mahagonny there are moments of nausea, helplessness and despair. 5. The men of Mahagonny are heard replying to God's inquiries as to the cause of their sinful life. 6. Lovely Mahagonny crumbles to nothing before your eyes'. Although we have none of Brecht's characteristic notes and schemes other than this to show how the opera was planned, the basis of the work is fairly clear. On the one hand there were the songs taken over from the Songspiel version, together with part of Mahagonny Song no. 4 and seven other pre-existing poems, which the collaborators now cut, changed and threaded together to make the backbone of the opera. On the other there was this new framework with its apocalyptic message deriving apparently from Brecht's discarded plan for *The Flood* or *Collapse of the Paradise City Miami*, which originally had nothing directly to do with the Mahagonny myth. The result was the libretto script which is now in the archives of Universal-Edition, Weill's publishers. This antedates not only the version which Brecht published in the *Versuche* in 1931, which is the basis for the *Gesammelte Werke* text which we reproduce, but also the piano score of 1929. It is entitled simply *Mahagonny*, 'opera in 3 acts by Kurt Weill. Text by Bert Brecht'.

This script gives the characters as Widow Leokadja Begbick, Fatty der Prokurist, Trinity Moses (identified as a bass), Jimmy Mahonney, Fresserjack (or Guzzlerjack), Sparbüchsenbilly (Piggy-Bank Billy), Alaskawolfjoe and Jenny Smith. Of these only Jimmy and Billy are taken over from the Songspiel, though the name Jenny occurs in a rough draft of a 'Mahagoni' song in one of Brecht's notebooks of 1922–23. The piano score of 1929 amends Jimmy to Jim Mahoney (with the normal single 'n'), drops Jenny's surname and adds Tobby Higgins, noting that he can be doubled with Jack. Auden and Kallman in their translation improved on this by making Jenny's name Jones (presumably because Jack or Jake is also named Smith) and Jimmy's Gallagher (presumably because Mǎhǒnĕy with three syllables will not do for Anglo-Saxons, let alone Irishmen). Just about that time, however, Weill decided that 'the use of American names . . . risks establishing a wholly false idea of Americanism, Wild West or suchlike', so that with Brecht's concurrence a note was added to the full score saying:

> In view of the fact that those amusements of man which can be had for money are always and everywhere the same, and since the amusement town of Mahagonny is thus international in the broadest sense, the names of the leading characters can be changed into the customary [i.e., local] forms at any given time. The following names are therefore recommended for German performances: Willy (for Fatty), Johann Ackermann (for Jim), Jakob Schmidt (for Jack O'Brien [actually the name of one of the world middleweight champions about whom Brecht wrote a poem in 1927]), Sparbüchsenheinrich (for Bill), Josef Lettner (for Joe).

These German names are to be found in *Versuche 2*, where the work is described as 'an attempt at epic opera, a depiction of mores'. However, Brecht now (see p. xvi) made Ackermann Paul, not Johann, though he is always the latter in performance.

The various incorporated poems, including the Mahagonny songs, will be given in full in the volume of *Songs and Poems from Plays* currently being prepared. They are, in brief:

Alabama Song (scene 2)
On the cities (scene 3)
Mahagonny Song no. 4 (scene 3, refrain only)
Mahagonny Song no. 1 (scene 4)
The Johnny-doesn't-want-to-be-human Song (scene 8)
Against being deceived (scene 11 in our text, scene 20 in piano score)
Blasphemy (scene 11)
The Lovers (scene 14)
Mahagonny Song no. 2 (scene 16)
Tahiti (scene 16)
Jenny's Song (scene 16)
Benares Song (scene 19 of piano score, later cut)

Mahagonny Song no. 3 (scene 19)
Poem on a Dead Man (scene 20)

There was also a discarded 'Chewing-gum Song'. How all these were treated in order to work them into the opera will be discussed in the notes on individual scenes which follow.

These are based on a comparison of the typescript libretto (which bears no signs of correction or amendment by Brecht), the piano score (1929) and the final *Versuche* text of 1931, which has subsequently remained unchanged. Since Auden and Kallman's translation of the opera was made from the piano score, we quote variant passages from the latter in their version. It can be found in its original form in Brecht: *The Rise and Fall of the City of Mahagonny*, edited by A. R. Braunmuller and published by David R. Godine, Boston 1976.

2. THE OPERA: NOTES ON INDIVIDUAL SCENES
Scene 1

In the typescript and the piano score (and accordingly in the original Auden–Kallman version) the stage directions are as under. Note however that Auden–Kallman's 'screen' is a mistranslation of Brecht's *Gardine* or flimsy curtain hung from wires 'not more than 2½ metres' (i.e. about eight feet) above the stage.

> *The place of the conventional curtain is taken by a small white screen suspended on both sides on metal wires about a yard above the stage. On this screen appear all the projections of the scene titles. As the music begins, a warrant for the arrest of Ladybird Begbick, Trinity Moses and Henry Wilson alias Fatty The Bookie, appears on the screen. The charges are: Robbery with Violence, Forgery and Fraud. Under this is printed: All Three are Fugitives from Justice. Their photographs then appear. Then, moving across this projection in red letters the title of the first scene: The Founding of the City of Mahagonny, otherwise known as Suckerville.*
> *The screen divides in the centre and opens inwards. Projection No. 1. appears on the backcloth: a desert landscape. A large, battered truck rolls on to the stage; the motor splutters and dies; the truck stops. Trinity Moses climbs out of the driver's seat and peers under the hood; Fatty peers out from the back of the truck.*

The 'As-You-Like-It Tavern' (of A/K following the piano score) later became the 'Rich Man's Arms Hotel'. This solo by Begbick (starting on p. 4) was originally termed 'Aria' in the script. The ending of her immediately preceding speech (from 'This is the spot' to 'settled') was added by A/K and is not in the German texts, while 'Girls for the asking' is literally 'Girls and boys'.

Scene 2

According to the piano score this is to be played before the half-height curtain (A/K's 'screen'). It consists of the Alabama Song originally written in English by Elisabeth Hauptmann and provided with a rudimentary tune by Brecht. The piano score omits the second verse, which originally had 'girl' rather than 'boy' throughout but was changed on the script and on Weill's MS score. We have followed the later reading, which has been observed ever since, and disregarded A/K's amendment of 'pretty boy' to 'Mister Right' and of 'boys' in the penultimate line of this verse to 'misters'.

Scene 3

In the typescript there was to be an opening projection 'showing a view of the city of New York and also the photographs of a lot of men'. In the piano score the former was amended to literally 'a city of millions'. The initial four-line chorus was published as a poem in *Simplicissimus* for 6 September 1927 under the title 'On the Cities'; later Brecht wanted to take it into the *Devotions*. The duet by Fatty and Moses which follows, according to the Weill–Neher 'Suggestions', was to be sung into a microphone. With 'But once you puff' (p. 7) it takes up the refrain of Mahagonny Song no. 4.

Scene 4

Is again performed before the half-curtain, and consists of Mahagonny Song no. 1.

Scene 5

The script has Trinity Moses putting up pictures of nudes, not simply of 'girls' (p. 11). It calls Jenny's song 'Have you thought at all' (p. 12) her 'Arietta' and words it slightly differently; thus in the verse starting 'Jenny Jones from Oklahoma' the third line reads 'I have been in the cold cities'. Doubtless seeing some inconsistency with the earlier 'My home is Havana' A/K give the alternatives 'Jenny Jones. Havana, Cuba' and 'Jenny Jones. From Havana' – the latter as part of a spoken quatrain to run on:

> I got here just about nine weeks ago.
> I used to live in the big cities down there.
> I do anything that's asked of me.

Also in the script the solo and chorus following straight on from there, starting 'I know you Jimmies, Jimmies, Jimmies from Alaska well' is separated off and headed 'Song', with the six girls joining in after 'what Mahagonny has to sell'. All this is given its present wording in the piano score, which has a different setting of the Arietta from that now used. Weill subsequently rewrote this song for Lotte Lenya to sing in the Berlin production of 1931.

Scene 6

Script and piano score specify that this is to be played before the half-curtain, on which is projected a plan of the city.

Scene 7

According to Drew the Tavern's name was changed to Hotel zum Reichen Mann (or The Rich Man's Arms) a few weeks before the Leipzig première.

The script divides Begbick's opening speech into verse lines and makes it end after 'I saw them there' with 'They're taking their money away with them!'. In her cantabile solo starting 'I too was once' (p. 17) instead of 'And it was love' the script has 'And it was the future'.

Scene 8

In script and piano score this starts with the same projection as scene 5. Jim's solo 'I think I will eat my old felt hat' (p. 19) is headed 'Song' on the script and derives from an earlier 'Johnny-willkeinmenschsein Song' which evidently antedates the naming of the characters. It is said by Werner Otto to derive from an unidentified record of a song in English. It had a melody by Brecht, a middle verse which went:

> I think I had better get rid of my woman
> I think she and I are through.
> And why should a man be stuck with his woman
> When he's stuck for money too?

– and a longer refrain, taking in all that follows the present second (Arkansas) verse from 'You've learned' right down to 'What is it man was born for?' In script, piano score and A/K version this follows each of the two verses.

Scene 9

The script introduces this scene by a title in 'giant flaming letters' saying 'SENSATION!' In our version A/K have added extensively to the inscriptions specified in the stage direction, and also signed each of them with Begbick's initials. Following the piano score they include a lot of repetition ('Hold me, hold me back! Hold me, hold me back! Hold me, hold me back' etc.) which the published texts dispense with and which we have accordingly cut. We have also followed Brecht in going straight into Jim's 'Deep in the woods' solo and omitting Jake's heartfelt 'This is the *real* immortal art!' which follows the introductory piano solo (derived from 'The Maiden's Prayer') in A/K and the piano score.

After 'The rivers jammed with floating ice' (p. 22) and Jim's three lines following, the script has a different version of the rest of the scene, as follows:

BEGBICK:
   If only those stupid idiots

Would stay put in Alaska
For all they want is to disturb
Our peace, our concord.

JENNY:

Jimmy, listen to me
And put your knife away

BEGBICK:

What is it you want?
Catch a fish and be happy
Smoke a cigar and forget
Your crappy Alaska.

THE GIRLS:

Put your knife back in your belt again!

CHORUS OF MEN:

Quiet! Quiet!

JAKE, JOE, BILL:

Jimmy, put your knife away!
Jimmy, be a gentleman!

JIM:

Hold me back
Or something nasty'll happen!

CHORUS *mocking*:

We know these Jimmies, Jimmies, Jimmies from Alaska well:
They have it worse in winter than the dead have.
But you get rich in hell. But you get rich in hell.

JIM *shouting*:

For there's no life here!

CHORUS *general tumult*:

Throw him out!
*At this point the stage lights go out. Sudden deathly hush. On the
background in big writing 'Hurricane over Florida!!' If possible to be
followed by 160 feet of film with shots of typhoons.*

SINGLE VOICES:

A hurricane!!
A typhoon!!!
A hurricane over Florida threatening Mahagonny!!!!!!
The darkness lightens somewhat.

CHORUS *bursting forth*:

No! Not utter destruction!

Our golden Joytown will be lost!
For the raging storm hangs over the mountains:
We shall die, drown in the waters of death.
O is there no wall to shelter us now?
O is there no cavern which will hide us?
Chorus rushes out. Begbick, Moses, Fatty and Jim remain.
MOSES:
Lock the doors!
Take the money to the cellar.
BEGBICK:
Oh, don't bother
It doesn't matter.
Jim laughs.

Scene 10

The script accordingly makes our scene 10 the concluding part
of the previous scene. The piano score separates it off exactly as
now, except that there is a note soon after the second projection,
saying 'Thereafter typhoon scenes can be shown, using scenic or
filmic means: storms, water, collapsing buildings, men and animals
fleeing etc.'.

Scene 11 [10 in script]

Script locates this 'Inside the As-You-Like-It Tavern' as in
scene 7. It omits Jenny's repeat of 'O moon of Alabama' (p. 25)
which is now sung over the top of Jake's solo, gives this solo
to the trio Jake–Joe–Bill, and shortens it, omitting the last line.
Then after Begbick's 'So you think I was wrong to forbid anything' (p. 30) Jim's answer (in verse) is:

Yes. Now I am cheerful
I would rather smash up your chairs
And your lamp
And your glasses must be destroyed.
He does so.
The hurricane will not pay you for them
But I will.

Here.
Take this.

Begbick's answer was then addressed to him only and to be sung on top of a repeat of 'We need no raging hurricane' etc. by the other three men. The script also provides a different ending to the scene after Jim's four lines starting 'You are free, I say, if you dare' (p. 31), cutting straight from 'If it's prohibited' to his repeat of 'As you make your bed' six lines later. There is then no chorus, and Jenny says:

> Be quiet, boys
> If they hear us we'll be lynched.
>
> JIM: No, we're going to stop being quiet from now on.
> *He smashes the boards announcing prohibitions.*

> *Lights dim down. Projection at the back: Mahagonny on the point of destruction, illuminated with blood-red rays. From the darkness we hear the chorus of Mahagonnyites, interrupted by the subversive songs of Jimmy and his friends: let each one do just what he likes, etc. The 'As you make your bed' song becomes increasingly dominant, and is eventually taken up by the entire chorus. The singing stops, the projection disappears, till all that can be seen in the background is a geographical sketch with an arrow slowly approaching Mahagonny, showing the hurricane's path.*

The piano score has the scene as now, except that it puts Jim's solo 'Dreams have all one ending' (p. 28) in the last scene but one, just before his execution. This was also followed by Auden/ Kallman. The present placing of the song seems to have been decided without Weill's agreement.

This song comes from a poem of about 1920 which had been included in the *Devotions* under the title 'Against Deception' but was earlier called 'Lucifer's Evening Song'. Jim's other solo which succeeds this in our text ('If you see a thing', p. 29) forms part of the 'Reader for Those Who Live in Cities' cycle of 1926–27, and was published as such in 1960 under the title 'Blasphemy'.

Scene 12 [11 in script]

This opens the second Act of the opera (see script and piano score). In the script the stage directions begin as now, but the first place mentioned is not the seemingly fictitious Atsena but Miami. The Auden–Kallman version groups the three loudspeaker announcements thus:

LOUDSPEAKER:
The hurricane is now approaching Atsena at a speed of one hundred and twenty miles an hour. In Pensacola, eleven thousand are reported dead or missing.
The hurricane has reached Atsena. Atsena totally destroyed.
The hurricane is making straight for Mahagonny. It is now only three minutes away.

Then as our text, except that the word 'Loudspeaker' is omitted.

Scene 13 [12 in script]

The script puts the opening chorus as part of the preceding scene, but introduces it by the same projected titles as now. It is however not sung by the chorus proper but by the four friends, in front of the half-curtain. The piano score has it as now, but with the wording bowdlerised to read 'Zweitens kommt die Liebe dran', instead of 'Zweitens kommt der Liebesakt'. Auden/Kallman follow the former reading. The two musicians of Brecht's stage direction are there to play zither and bandoneon, a type of accordion, in the accompaniment to Jake's solo.

At the end of the scene the script makes the friends appear without Jake to sing the 'One means to eat' etc. refrain. From now on however the order of the lines rotates. Thus it is now love first, followed by ring, drink and 'Fourth means to eat all you are able'; then at the end of the next scene it is ring, drink, eating and love; then at the end of the boxing scene, when only Jim and Bill are left to sing it, drink, eating, love and ring, in that order; then finally when Jim is arrested at the end of the next scene it is back to normal, with the whole chorus singing 'Now you can eat all you are able' and so on.

Scene 14 [13 in script]

The script shows that this was originally to be considerably tighter and more realistic. Its opening stage direction is:

> *The word* LOVE *in huge letters on a background with, in front of it, right, the Mandlay* [*sic*] *Brothel with a queue of men lining up. The three friends join the queue. Erotic pictures are immediately shown on a canvas screen. Meanwhile Begbick's voice is heard off.*

Begbick's and the men's opening lines are as now, but the stage directions differ: the men '*murmur after her*' and instead of the room getting dark '*The men are getting impatient*' before their 'Get to it soon!' etc. From there on the rest of the scene is different. First Trinity Moses

> *steps out in front of the brothel.*
> We thank all you gents for the patience you've been showing.
> I'm told that another three gents can shortly go in.
> Experience will tell you: to savour love at its best
> Every client needs a moment to rest.

> *Moses ushers out three gentlemen and lets three in. The others go on waiting. The three who have been ushered out rejoin the queue. Further pictures are shown, and Begbick's voice is again heard.*

BEGBICK:
> Let the tips of your fingers
> Stroke the tips of her breasts
> And wait for the quivering of her flesh.

THE MEN *murmur after her*:

[the same words, then] '*the men become impatient*' once more and repeat their 'Mandelay' chorus. Moses '*reemerges from the brothel*' and again sings his four lines. Then

> *Moses ushers out the three gentlemen just admitted and lets in Jim, Bill and Joe, who have jostled their way to the front. The remainder are once again shown pictures.*

BEGBICK'S VOICE:
> Introducto pene frontem in fronte ponens requiescat.

THE MEN *in frantic impatience*:
Mandalay won't glow forever below such a moon.
Hurry, the juicy moon is green and slowly setting.
The three friends are ushered out and step in front of the half-curtain,
which closes.

They close the scene by singing the next round of the refrain.

This version of the scene, which omits the Crane Duet (p. 36), was originally set by Weill as shown in the revised 1969 edition of the piano score which David Drew has edited for Universal-Edition. In the script however there is also an alternative version marked 'for the libretto'. Here, and in the piano score followed by A/K, the opening stage direction has the Men 'leaning their backs against' the platform and 'sitting on a long bench'. The scene follows much as we have it, with the lights going up and down in the room until Jim and Jenny are discovered there and go into the Crane Duet. In the piano score of 1929 not only is the duet fully composed but everything before it (from the opening of the half-curtain at the start of the scene) is marked as an optional cut. Within this all Moses's lines, the script's stage directions showing the admission of three men at a time, and Begbick's remark in Latin have anyway been omitted, leaving purely orchestral passages where Moses had been meant to sing. Thereafter the refrain 'Get to it soon' lost its last three lines in the printed versions (though we retain A/K's rendering of them). Two other lines following Jenny's 'For nowhere' (p. 37) and translated by A/K

So all true lovers are,
True lovers are, true lovers are

were likewise cut.

The Duet is thought by Drew to derive from one of Brecht's love sonnets, in which case it could hardly be earlier than 1925; but no such poem is known. It was published as a poem in his *A Hundred Poems* (1951) under the title 'The Lovers'. Weill's setting dates from October 1929.

For the 1931 Berlin production the first part of the scene, in its bowdlerised version, was restored and the duet cut instead. At some later point Weill decided that the duet would go best in the last Act, but he never prescribed a place for it and there is no evidence that he discussed the problem with Brecht. The revised piano score of 1969 suggests putting it in scene 19 in lieu of the spoken dialogue from Jim's 'Why, you're wearing a white dress' (p. 58) to Jenny's 'Kiss me, Jimmy' (p. 59).

Scene 15 [14 in script]

Apart from the rotation of lines in the final refrain, and the effects of the musical setting, this scene has scarcely changed since the first script.

Scene 16 [15 in script]

In the script the stage direction omits all mention of playing billiards. Where our text has 'MEN' it has 'JIM AND THE MEN'; the piano score and A/K however have a quartet of JIM, BILL, FATTY and MOSES. Their song 'Mahagonny sure was swell' is Mahagonny Song no. 2, which the script gives them to sing as printed in the *Devotions*, but without verse 2 and its refrain. In the piano score and our text verse 2 and refrain follow verse 1, while the refrain of verse 3 ('Stay-at-homes do very well') concludes the scene. For the Leipzig production however there was a cut from the first 'But at least they saw the moon' (p. 43) as far as Begbick's 'Time to settle the bill, gentlemen' (p. 44), and this was accepted by the composer from then on.

Script and piano score (followed by Auden–Kallman) have Jim, '*dead-drunk*', bawling the song 'Pour cognac down the toilet and flush it' (p. 45) which uses verses 1, 3 and 2 (in that order) of the poem 'Tahiti' which Brecht wrote about 1921. In the Men's chorus that follows ('Death now is nigh!') and continues under the spoken exchange between Jenny, Jim and Bill, Auden and Kallman have written new text rather than repeat phrases as in Weill's setting; the whole chorus then reads:

Death now is nigh!
Now black as pitch the sky
The white-caps high.

The dark draws in
And heaven is heaven with menace
Black, black as sin!
Black, black as sin
Black, black as sin
The menace of darkness draws in!

'Stormy the night', of which one quatrain follows, was first cited in *In the Jungle of Cities* (see *Collected Plays 1*, p. 451) and comes from the nineteenth-century ballad 'Das Seemannslos' ('The Sailor's Lot'), which Brecht evidently knew from his childhood. In the contemporary English version by Arthur J. Lamb it is known as 'Asleep on the Deep', and the corresponding quatrain there reads

Stormy the night and the waves roll high
Bravely the ship doth ride.
Hark! while the light-house bell's solemn cry
Rings over the sullen tide.

Auden presumably did not know it, or it might well have been in his anthology *The Poet's Tongue*. It was set to music by H. W. Petrie in 1895.

In the script Jenny's solo 'Let me tell you' (p. 48) is headed 'Jenny's Song'. Besides some minor verbal differences it has a third verse, which was apparently never set, but goes:

I can't go with you in future, Jimmy
Yes, Jimmy, it's sad for me.
You'll still be my favourite all right, but
You're a waste of my time, you see.
I must use the little time that's left me
Jimmy
Or I'll lose my grip on it.
You're only young once, and that's
Not enough.
I tell you, Jimmy
I am shit.

Oh, Jimmy, you know what my mother told me . . .

– and so on as we have it. Thereafter the scene ends almost immediately, thus:

BEGBICK:
   Again I say:
   Pay!
JIM *says nothing.*
BEGBICK:
   Then let the police take him away!

– followed by Moses's lines (p. 49) and then the refrain, this time by all the men, starting 'Now you can eat all you are able'. This was cut by Weill (see the 1969 revised piano score).

A version of Jenny's song, starting 'When I put on my wedding dress' is included in a fragmentary *Threepenny Opera* scene set in Polly's room. It has a melody in Brecht's notation.

Scene *17* [16 in script]

The script has Jim sitting shackled in a little cage, past which the chorus of the previous scene pass as they leave the stage. His solo is headed 'Jimmy's Aria'. In the piano score (followed by Auden/Kallman) he '*lies in the forest, one foot chained to a tree*'. For the Kassel production of 12 March 1930 the aria was shifted to the next scene, its place being taken by 'Dreams have all one ending' (now in our scene 11) from the penultimate scene. Weill found this made a more effective ending to the second Act, but for the Berlin production he reduced it to one verse only and reset it for chorus (or male chorus) leaving it in full in the penultimate scene.

Scene *18* [17 in script]

According to script and piano score this starts the third Act. The former specifies a projected title saying 'Like the rest of the world's law courts, that of Mahagonny sentences people if they are poor'. The first defendant then is Joe, who is charged in Moses's words

   With premeditated murder of 5 men
   Done to test a newly purchased revolver.

> Accused, you have destroyed
> 5 human lives in full bloom.

Then 'Never yet' etc., as now. Jim's offence, however, is announced thus by Moses (p. 52):

> Second, the case of Jim Mahoney
> Indicted on account of
> Three bottles of whisky and a bar-rail
> He failed to pay for.

– 'bar-rail' being A/K's substitute for Brecht's word 'curtain-rod'. In A/K (following the piano score) the courtroom is not specifically located in a tent, and the first defendant's name is given (amended by them from Brecht's Tobby Higgins to Toby throughout).

After Bill's plea 'Of all those hanging around' etc. (p. 55) the script has the Men saying nothing, merely applauding and hissing. Moses, not Fatty, calls for 'Your verdict, august tribunal' (p. 56); while Begbick gives Jim four years in prison (rather than the four years' probation of the final text) for the seduction of an unnamed girl. Auden/Kallman (following the piano score) omit Begbick's sentence starting 'In view of' (p. 56) and add a stage direction at this point saying '*On the backcloth is projected the "Wanted" poster that was seen at the opening of Act One*'.

[Scene 19 in piano score only]

This was not in the script and was cut in the Leipzig production. It consisted of the Benares Song, which Elisabeth Hauptmann wrote in English in 1926, and which in Auden/Kallman's version goes thus. The original text is given in brackets where altered by them:

19

At this time a good many people in Mahagonny who wanted something different and better began dreaming of the city of Benares. But meanwhile Benares was visited by an earthquake.

Jenny, Begbick, Fatty, Bill, Moses and Toby enter in front of the screen [i.e. the half-curtain], *seat themselves on high bar-stools and drink ice-water: the Men read newspapers.*

BEGBICK:
There is no whiskey in this town   ['whisky' throughout]
JENNY:
No bar that doesn't get us down.
                           [There is no bar to sit us down.]
FATTY, BILL AND MOSES:
Oh!
BEGBICK *sentimentally*:
Where is the telephone?
FATTY, BILL AND MOSES:
Oh!
JENNY *urgently*:
Is there no telephone?   [Is here no telephone?]
MOSES:
O God, so help me, no.   [Oh Sir, God damn me, no.]
FATTY, TOBY AND BILL:
Oh!
JENNY AND BEGBICK:
Let's go, let's go   [Let's go to Benares]
To Benares where the sun is shining.
                           [Where the sun is shining.]
Let's go, let's go to Benares,   [Let's go to Benares]
To Benares, Johnny, let us go.   [Johnny, let us go.]

BEGBICK:
    There is no money in this land,
JENNY:
    No boy that's glad to shake your hand.
                        [There is no boy to shake with hands.]
etc., to:
    BILL AND MOSES:
    To Benares where the sun is shining.
    BEGBICK·
    There is no prize here we can win,
                        [There is not much fun on this star.]
JENNY:
    No door that lets us out or in.
                        [There is no door that is ajar.]
FATTY, BILL AND MOSES:
    Oh!
BEGBICK *sentimentally*:
    Where is the telephone?
FATTY, BILL AND MOSES:
    Oh!
JENNY *urgently*:
    Is there no telephone?
MOSES:
    No, no, goddamit, no!   [As before, to end of refrain.]
FATTY, TOBY AND BILL:
    Oh!
    *They find out from the papers about the earthquake in Benares. They
    jump to their feet in horror.*
ALL SIX:
    Worst of all,   [Worst of all, Benares]
    Benares is now reported perished in an earthquake!
                [Is said to have been perished by an earthquake.]
    O my dear Benares,   [Oh my good Benares!]
    Now where shall we go?   [Oh where shall we go?]

Scene 19 [18 in the script, 20 in the piano score and A/K]

The script has the opening stage direction as now, except that
instead of an electric chair being made ready '*On the right stands a*

makeshift gallows'. The white dress (p. 58) was black. Jim's speech leaving Jenny to Bill (p 59.) had an extra line: 'For *he* can live without fun'. Moses called 'Ready!' before they turned *'towards the place of execution'* (p. 59), and then asked after the 'One means to eat' refrain:

> Have you a last request?

JIM:
> Yes.
> I would like once again
> To hear the girls sing
> The song of the moon
> Of Alabama.

The girls sing the Alabama Song as Jim mounts the gallows.

MOSES:
> Have you anything else to say?

JIM:
> Yes.
> I would like
> You all not to let my horrible death
> Put you off living the way that suits you, carefree.
> For I too
> Am not sorry
> That I did
> What I wanted.
> Listen to my advice.
> *He climbs on a bucket, and as they fasten the noose round his neck he sings*

– all four verses of 'Dreams have all one ending' (as in our scene 11), after which Moses says 'Ready!' again, and there is a black-out. Then the half-curtain closes, and Jenny, Fatty, Moses and two un-named Men come out and sing Mahagonny Song no. 3 (God in Mahagonny). It is arranged as in our text, except for the omission of verse 2 (Mary Weeman etc.), and in the script it concludes the scene.

In the piano score there is no repeat of the Alabama Song; so Jim's speech 'Yes. / I would like /' etc., now printed as prose,

follows directly after Moses's 'Have you a last request?'. Auden/
Kallman here substitute the following speech, based very loosely
on the *Versuche* text:

> JIM: Yes. At last I realize what a fool I've been. I came to this
> city believing there was no happiness which money could not
> procure. That belief has been my downfall. For now I am
> about to die without ever having found the happiness I
> looked for. The joy I bought was no joy; the freedom I was
> sold was no freedom. I ate and remained unsatisfied; I drank
> and became all the thirstier. I'm damned and so, probably, are
> most of you. Give me a glass of water.
> *Jim stands in front of the electric chair. During the following, he is
> being prepared for execution.*

– the following being his singing of 'Dreams have all one ending'.
After it the piano score (which A/K again abandon here) ends
quickly with:

> *Jim sits on the electric chair. They put the helmet over his head.*
> MOSES:
> Ready!
> *Black-out.*

'God in Mahagonny' then becomes the beginning of the following
scene, where it is sung before the half-curtain by Jenny, Fatty,
Bill, Moses and a fourth man.

Jim's final speech of remorse (p. 62), which Auden and Kallman
put in the place of the earlier 'Yes. / I would like /' etc., derives
from a letter from Weill to his publisher dated 25 March 1930 (i.e.
just after the Leipzig and Kassel performances) saying that some
such speech was needed 'for the understanding of the whole
thing'; it was wrong for Jim to remain unrepentant.

When or why Brecht decided to shift 'Dreams have all one
ending' back to scene 11 is unknown, though clearly it was before
Versuche 2 (1930) went to press. For the Kassel performance Weill
had moved it forward, but only to precede our scene 17 (q.v.),
while for the Berlin production he decided it was needed in its
original position.

The opening inscription is rather freely translated by A/K, who
omit the final phase cited on p. xx.

Scene 20 [19 in script, 21 in piano score, 22 in A/K]

In the script this is preceded by a projected inscription saying

NEXT DAY THE WHOLE OF MAHAGONNY WAS ON FIRE. THE BURIAL OF J. MAHONEY THE LUMBERJACK BECAME A TURNING-POINT IN THE CITY'S HISTORY. DO NOT BE RESENTFUL BUT OBSERVE THIS VAST DEMONSTRATION, WHICH IS BEING STAGED IN THE PUBLIC INTEREST.

Then the half-curtain opens, showing the projection of Mahagonny in flames and the people of the city gathering upstage with '*placards, signs and banners*'. The only words here are those of the chorus 'Why, though, did we need a Mahagonny?' as at the end of our scene 1, which is taken from the finale of the Songspiel. They are followed by a stage direction saying:

After the song the crowd starts moving in small groups, each carrying its placards etc. and marching in a big semicircle from back left down past the footlights to back right. The placards say roughly:
1. For the natural order of things
2. For the natural disorder of things
3. For the corruptibility of our courts
4. For the incorruptibility of our courts
5. For freedom for the rich
6. For freedom for everybody
7. For the unjust division of temporal goods
8. For the just division of spiritual goods
9. For the underhandedness of the human race
10. (*A giant placard*) Against the human race
In the middle of the procession comes a group carrying Jim's coffin. The play ends with huge songs as the demonstrators continue their constant marching.

Curtain.

End of the opera.

In the piano score the '*stage darkens*' after the conclusion of 'God in Mahagonny' (which, it will be remembered, opens the final scene there), and is followed by a projection. This introduces a separate scene 22 in Auden/Kallman's version, which otherwise follows the piano score and goes thus:

22

In these days, because of the unheard-of rise in prices, gigantic riots broke out in Mahagonny, preluding the end of Suckerville. The rioters carried the body of Jimmy Gallagher in procession

The screen opens. On the backcloth one sees Mahagonny in flames. Begbick, Fatty and Moses stand downstage. After they sing, groups of Demonstrators enter in continual succession until the close.

BEGBICK, FATTY AND MOSES:
>Why, though, did we need a Mahagonny?
>Because this world is a foul one
>With neither charity
>Nor peace nor concord,
>Because there's nothing
>To build any trust upon.

GROUP OF MEN *enter bearing Jim's hat and cane on velvet cushions*:
>We need no raging hurricane,
>We need no bolt from the blue:
>There's no havoc which they might have done
>That we cannot better do.

A SECOND GROUP *enter with Jim's ring, revolver and cheque-book*:
>As you make your bed so you lie on it,
>The bed can be old or brand-new:
>So if someone must kick, that is my part,
>And another get kicked, that part's for you.
>As you make your bed so you lie on it
>And you buy the sheets for it too:

So if someone must kick, that is my part,
And another get kicked, that's for you.
BEGBICK, FATTY AND MOSES:
Why, though, did we need a Mahagonny?
Because this world is a foul one
With neither charity
Nor peace nor concord,
Because there's nothing
To build any trust upon.
JENNY AND SOME GIRLS *enter carrying Jim's shirt*:
Oh, moon of Alabama
We now must say good-bye
We've lost our good old mama
And must have dollars, oh, you know why.
Oh, moon of Alabama
We now must say good-bye
We've lost our good old mama
And must have dollars, oh, you know why.
Bill enters at the head of another Group of Men.
BILL:
You can bring vinegar – to him
You can wipe his forehead – for him
You can find surgical forceps
You can pull the tongue from his gullet
Can't do anything to help a dead man.
BILL'S GROUP:
Can't do anything to help a dead man.
Various placards are displayed. They run more or less:
For the natural order of things
For the natural disorder of things
For the freedom of the rich
For the freedom of all
For the unjust division of temporal goods
For the just division of spiritual goods
For pure love
For brute stupidity
Can't do anything to help a dead man.
Moses enters at the head of a new group.
You can talk good sense – to him

You can bawl oaths – at him
You can just leave him lying
You can take care – of him
Can't give orders, can't lay down any law to a dead man.

MOSES'S AND BILL'S GROUPS:

Can't do anything to help a dead man
No one can do nothing for a dead man.

Begbick enters with a third group that is carrying Jim's body.

BEGBICK:

You can put coins in his hand – for him
You can dig a hole – by him
You can stuff that hole – with him
You can heap a shovelful – on him
Can't do anything to help a dead man.

BILL, MOSES AND THREE GROUPS OF MEN:

Can't do anything to help a dead man
Can't do anything to help a dead man.

*Fatty enters with a fourth group. They carry an enormous placard:
For the re-establishment of the golden age.*

FATTY:

You can talk about the glory of his heyday
You can also forget his days completely
You can change his old shirt for a clean one
Can't do anything to help a dead man.

ALL:

No one can do nothing for a dead man
Can't help him or you or me or no one.

Curtain

This 'Poem on a Dead Man' also formed part of Weill's *Berliner Requiem*, written in the winter of 1928–29. In the version which Brecht had written some four and a half years earlier its fourth verse went

You can talk about the glory of his heyday
You can also forget his days completely
You can lead a better life, lead a worse one
Can't do anything to help a dead man.

– without the opera's final line.